Different Blood: The Vampire as Alien

By Margaret L. Carter

Different Blood: The Vampire as Alien
Copyright 2019, 2024 Margaret L. Carter
Writers Exchange E-Publishing
PO Box 372
ATHERTON QLD 4883

Cover Art by: Jatin

Published by Writers Exchange E-Publishing
http://www.writers-exchange.com

Dedication

Dedicated to Suzy McKee Charnas, creator of Dr. Weyland, the ultimate "alien vampire."

In addition, I owe special thanks to S. T. Joshi for his editorial guidance.

Introduction

Stepping Sideways

Vampires in science fiction, like other alien races, often function as a distorted reflection of ourselves, illuminating the human predicament by contrast. When Ransom, the hero of C. S. Lewis' *Out of the Silent Planet,* visits Mars, he encounters three sentient species rather than one. A Martian sage expresses surprise upon learning that Earth harbors only one intelligent species. He concludes, "Your thought must be at the mercy of your blood... For you cannot compare it with thought that floats on a different blood" (103). Lewis' aliens place a high value upon communion between members of different species.

The natives of Lewis' Mars are not vampires, yet his works do cast light upon the literary motif of the vampire as alien. *Out of the Silent Planet* offers a deliberate contrast to the older image of extraterrestrials (specifically Martians) embodied in such creatures as the vampiric aliens of H. G. Wells' *War of the*

Worlds. As Lewis remarks in the dialogue "Unreal Estates", "most of the earlier [science fiction] stories start from the...assumption that we, the human race, are in the right, and everything else is ogres" (147). Wells' novel of Martian hostile invaders who consume the blood of human captives falls into this category (though Wells' characterization of his Martians is a bit more ambiguous than the term "ogres" implies). In *Out of the Silent Planet*, Lewis offers a more benign model of the first-contact situation. The antagonist in this novel, influenced by Wellsian science fiction, kidnaps Ransom and brings him to Mars as a human sacrifice, under the misapprehension that "the *eldil* [angelic spirit] drinks blood" (121). Explaining his predicament to the ruling *eldil* of Mars, Ransom says, "I was in terrible fear. The tellers of tales in our world make us think that if there is any life beyond our own air it is evil" (121). Through his interaction with the natives, he learns the error of this belief. His initial fear of the Martians yields to a desire to communicate with them, leading to friendship. Significantly for the theme of rapport between human minds and "thought that floats on a different blood", Ransom is a philologist, a specialist in communication. The tension between fear of (and consequent hostility to) the alien Other and the drive toward inter-species understanding dominates "vampire as alien" fiction.

In "Unreal Estates" Lewis himself cites an instance of friendly contact between a human protagonist and a quasi-vampiric extraterrestrial, from Zenna Henderson's short story "Food to All Flesh". Henderson's character, Padre Manuel, finding a spaceship in his pasture, tries to aid the hungry alien, a huge, sleek, fanged female accompanied by a litter of cubs. The visitor tests every available source of nourishment, including a variety of foods provided by Manuel, without finding anything her kind can digest. One of the starving cubs bites Manuel, and immediately, "Its little silver tongue came out and licked around happily and it went to sleep" (81). In the face of the knowledge that human flesh and blood can feed the alien cubs, Manuel neither fights nor flees when the mother seizes him. She, in turn, releases him, gathers up her young, and departs in her ship. Lacking any common language, human and alien nevertheless attain a rapport that supersedes their differences. Despite their "different blood", they share a common ethic grounded in reverence for life. Henderson's story and *The War of the Worlds* represent two extremes in fictional treatment of aliens (vampires as well as other types). A tone of hostility and paranoia prevails in earlier literature but also survives alongside the more sympathetic rendering of nonhuman characters in contemporary works.

These two contrasting attitudes--fear/hostility and the desire to understand the Other--as applied to vampire fiction are analyzed by Jacqueline Lichtenberg in an essay entitled "Vampire with Muddy Boots". She classifies the two ways of dealing with "monsters" as the horror approach and the science fiction approach. In horror "the Unknown is a menace which is a menace because it's a menace. In sf [science fiction], the Unknown is a menace because we don't understand it yet... In sf, understanding, either intellectual or emotion [sic], or maybe both, is the key to the solution of the problem" (4). Not only does a natural (science fiction) rather than supernatural (horror) rationale for the "monster" provide the opportunity for human characters to understand rather than fear him, this approach also allows the nonhuman character free will and the possibility of moral choice, bounded by the limitations of flesh and blood. "A true supernatural force," Lichtenberg points out, "doesn't suffer the inconvenience of slogging through cold wet mud. And as a result, such an entity doesn't grow spiritually, in character or relationships" (5). Her own fictional vampires, in contrast, deal with moral quandaries and strive for emotional connection both among themselves and with human companions. She envisions "a world in which each and every individual has a fighting chance provided they're willing to...step outside their cultural straight jackets [sic] to deal with the Unknown on a friendly basis" (5). Lichtenberg declares her goal as a novelist to be "to step sideways into another universe and become another person for awhile" (5). In general, "vampire as alien" fiction typically invites the reader to "step sideways" into the consciousness of a not-quite-human being, who offers a fresh perspective on the human condition.

The alien Other sometimes offers this insight by foregrounding separation rather than connection between human and nonhuman. Fear and hostility overshadow works that view the vampire from outside, as the "Unknown...which is a menace," in Lichtenberg's words. Many contemporary vampire stories, on the other hand, portray the monster as marginalized outsider with sympathy rather than hostility, grounding the narrative in his or her consciousness rather than the human viewpoint. Anne Rice, for instance, sees the vampire as "a metaphor for the outsider" (Anya Martin, 38). She attributes much of the appeal of her vampires to this metaphorical resonance. She made Lestat a rock star because "rock singers are symbolic outsiders" who are "expected to be completely wild, completely unpredictable, and completely themselves, and they are rewarded for that" (38). According to Rice, in contemporary American culture "all of the different transgressive ways of doing things have merged into the mainstream" (Riley, 56). In this kind of atmosphere, behavior that would have provoked ostracism in Bram Stoker's time can indeed be "rewarded", so that the very traits for which the characters in *Dracula* fear and loathe vampires become grounds for the glamorizing of vampires in today's fiction. Although supernatural and formerly human rather than literally alien, Rice's vampires behave and think like a separate species, free to "transgress" conventional human ethics and mores. Her vampires "are in the midst of everything, yet are completely cut off," and thereby "able to see things that human beings aren't able to see" (quoted in Ramsland, 337). Now no longer human, her vampires become "people outside life who can speak about it... They are able to perceive what the inside is better than those who are actually there" (337). Depending on the narrative perspective from which he or she is viewed, the marginalized Other may function as either positive or negative.

The identification of the vampire with the outsider is supported by Tobin Siebers' theory of superstition as "a symbolic activity, in which individuals of the same group mark one another as different". The stigmatizing of unconventional neighbors as witches, for instance, is "a form of accusation that effects social differentiation" (34). Superstition, thus, can function as a device for social control. Belief in the supernatural "represents individuals and groups as different from others in order to stratify violence and to create social hierarchies" (12). Historically, this view of supernaturalism is borne out by the fact that the upsurge in documented cases of supposed vampirism in the seventeenth century (also the peak of the witchcraft persecutions) coincides with territorial conflict among different branches of Christianity in Europe. On the individual level, many folklore traditions brand redheads as likely vampires, no doubt simply because of the relative rarity of that hair color. "The group represents individuals or other groups as different," according to Siebers, "for the purpose of creating a stable center around which to achieve unanimity" (40). Taken to the extreme, such exclusionary tactics constitute "the superstitious doubting of another's humanity" (34)--viewing the Other negatively as a direct consequence of his or her alienness.

Rosemary Jackson, similarly, suggests in her discussion of *Dracula* that the representatives of society's established order (Van Helsing and his allies) can maintain that order only by a radical act of exclusion, framing the vampire as wholly other, and the novel, in the process of this exclusion, "identifies the protean shadow of the 'other' as evil" (121). "In what we could call a supernatural economy," she comments, "otherness is transcendent, marvelously different from the human" (23). To those who embrace this kind of world-view, as observed by Fredric Jameson, "the concept of evil is at one with the concept of Otherness itself: evil characterizes whatever is radically different from me" (140). As symbolized by the vampire's inability to cast a reflection in a mirror, this viewpoint denies that the Other in any way reflects the self. This is the mind-set that rejects the Unknown as a menace because it is Unknown. Yet, conversely, the allure of the Other remains present even in works such as *Dracula*, which, as Jackson remarks, "engages with a...desire for and dismissal of transgressive energies" (118). Although the story culminates in "dismissal" of the forbidden "energies", it must first work through the "desire". The vampire, like other kinds of aliens, evokes fear, attraction, hostility, or fascination, sometimes all at once.

The tension between the allure and the threat of the Other is illuminated by James Tiptree's "And I Awoke and Found Me Here on the Cold Hill's Side". Though not a literal vampire story, it does involve a form of metaphorical vampirism. The dialogue within the text delivers a message that the narrator, listening to an embittered Ancient Mariner figure in the familiar spaceport bar of classic science fiction, hears as, "Never love an alien" (14). The old space-hand's warning, however, has a more profound truth to convey. The yearning to know aliens, says the stranger, drains Earth of resources both physical and spiritual, just as the Polynesians lost their own culture in yearning after European technology. "Our soul is leaking out," says the stranger. "We're bleeding to death!" (16). He explains the surrender to this metaphorical exsanguination in terms of "supernormal stimulus", the biological phenomenon that makes some birds reject their own eggs in favor of a larger, more colorful substitute. "Man is exogamous--all our history is one long drive to find and impregnate the stranger. Or get impregnated by him... For millions of years that kept the genes circulating. But now we've met aliens we can't screw, and we're about to die trying" (16). This drive, more than sexual, springs from "some cargo-cult of the soul. We're built to dream outwards" (17). The narrator, of course, hears the stranger's tirade without really listening. In the story's final paragraph he catches "a glimpse of two sleek scarlet shapes" and, obliviously eager to have his soul drained, hurries in pursuit of his "first real aliens" (17).

The drive to "dream outwards", often tempered or sharpened by awareness of the danger inherent in seeking communion with the Other, pervades contemporary fiction of the vampire as alien. In this work I mean by the term "alien" any vampire explained in science fiction terms as a naturally evolved creature, a member of a nonhuman sentient species, whether of earthly or extraterrestrial origin. In some narratives that explain vampirism as a mutation within a human line of descent, features of the "separate species" motif may appear. This survey will also discuss a few works that use the "disease" model of science fiction vampirism, since some of these (e.g., Richard Matheson's *I Am Legend*) portray their transmuted human characters as the founders of a new race.

The precise origin attributed to the "alien" vampire--whether extraterrestrial, an earthly species evolved separately from *Homo sapiens,* or a nonhuman offshoot from human forebears--matters less than his or her other distinguishing traits. These creatures may be solitary predators or gregarious members of a wolflike pack. They may be either animals driven by appetite alone, beings vastly superior to humanity in intelligence as well as strength and longevity, or simply unlike us, roughly equal to our own kind yet with different powers and limitations. In their relations with us, they may appear terrifying, fascinating, benevolent, or, most often, ambiguous. Psychiatrist Ernest Jones comments that the vampire of folklore is the most "over-determined" of superstitions, springing from a variety of roots in the human unconscious (98). It is therefore not surprising to find the literary vampire marked by an array of multifarious, sometimes contradictory characteristics and used for a wide range of different narrative purposes. As Ken Gelder observes, "*culturally,* this creature may be highly adaptable" and "can be made to appeal to or generate fundamental urges located somehow 'beyond' culture (desire, anxiety, fear), while simultaneously, it can stand for a range of meanings and positions *in* culture" (141, Gelder's emphasis).

Various literary vampires' individual traits necessarily both arise from and shape the thematic uses to which the respective authors put their alien predators. As already noted, some works, particularly the earlier ones, project fear and hatred onto external forces and use vampires as concrete embodiments of these forces. In later fiction, the vampire more often symbolizes the fascination of the Other. The narrative may also combine attraction and repulsion in the same entity, e.g., C. L. Moore's "Shambleau". Where an author portrays human-vampire relations as ambivalent, he or she may either split the threatening and benevolent aspects between two or more individual vampires or may combine these aspects in a single ambiguous character. Alien vampires may serve as metaphors for minority races or nonhuman animals, focusing on the importance of interracial tolerance and ecological responsibility. The vampire may also symbolize the outcast elements of human society, as Anne Rice's nonhuman characters, for instance, reflect the marginalized status of the gay community. As a predator at the top of the food chain, one element in the balance of nature, the vampire often stands in contrast to the wanton destruction perpetrated by human beings on their own kind; thus, by his or her moderate, morally neutral predation, the vampire foregrounds the wastefulness of human greed and violence.

Hence the vampire's otherness may cast light on what it means to be human. Many alien vampires either vainly wish to become human or fear the weakening effect of intimacy with, and consequent likeness to, their human prey. The vampire's attraction to and fear of human beings reflect the human characters' similar reactions to the vampire. Like Rice's Louis, allowing himself to be interviewed, and Lestat, becoming a celebrity in defiance of his own kind's law, alien vampires characteristically wish to disclose themselves to us. Rice imagines Lestat saying through his music, "I don't want to be an anonymous predatory shadow doomed to be misunderstood and only destroy" (Riley, 31). It is not surprising that the theme of interspecies communication dominates much of the fiction to be discussed in this survey. Such works fall under a new subgenre proposed by Jacqueline Lichtenberg, "Intimate Adventure", in which "partnership is the key to survival as well as happiness," and the stakes in the narrative's conflict "are not the possession of things or power over people; the stakes are happiness, fulfillment, and a worthwhile life" ("A Proposal for a New Genre Name," 68-69). The typical context is the exploration of a relationship between two radically unlike characters, an "Adventure" in which "one or both of the contestants locked into the struggle for intimacy have left a known, safe existence behind, either physically or emotionally" (69). In the most characteristic of these narratives, "a human meets a nonhuman person, and they must reach across the gulf between them" (69). Lichtenberg draws upon vampire fiction for many of her examples. In vampire Intimate Adventure, the danger of abandoning a "known, safe existence" to seek intimacy is particularly clear, since both parties to the mutual disclosure, human and alien, risk death.

Authors portray characters eager to embrace this risk because the desire to touch the mind of the Other expresses a perennial human longing. J. R. R. Tolkien identifies this yearning in "On Fairy Stories", asserting that fairy tales provide the imaginary "satisfaction of certain primordial human desires", among them the wish "to hold communion with other living things" (41). The talking animals prevalent in fairy tales embody the desire for this communion. Isolated from the nonhuman world, we find that "other creatures are like other realms with which Man has broken off relations, and sees now only from the outside at a distance" (84). Among the creations of literary fantasy, the vampire is uniquely suited to bridge this gulf. As Gelder summarizes the "transgressive" function of Gothic fiction in general, this kind of narrative "render[s] something simultaneously familiar and strange, recognised and unknowable" (47). Veiling an alien mind behind a human appearance, almost human but not quite, the vampire provides a view of the universe familiar enough for us to understand, yet skewed enough to infuse the known reality with the freshness of the unknown.

The scope of this study comprises vampires as natural (rather than supernatural) beings, conceptualized as members of another species, either humanoid or nonhumanoid, terrestrial or extraterrestrial. (Therefore, many of the groundbreaking vampire novels of the last three decades of the twentieth century, such as those of Anne Rice, Fred Saberhagen, and Chelsea Quinn Yarbro, and Kim Newman's alternate history Dracula series, are excluded because of their basis in the traditional supernatural model. Science fiction explanations of vampirism that do not characterize vampires as a separate species are also excluded.) Sometimes the point of origin is left unmentioned or ambiguous. Although some of the creatures to be discussed are either almost human or completely inhuman, we will find many gradations between the two extremes; the "humanoid / nonhumanoid" distinction is a continuum, not a sharp dichotomy. In the first chapter, I begin by analyzing the "alien" dimension of the definitive vampire novel, *Dracula*. Though Stoker's traditionally supernatural Undead Count lies outside the boundaries of the literally "alien", the novel's pivotal role in the history of vampire fiction makes its treatment of the Other important for the later evolution of the alien vampire motif. The first chapter then explores this motif as expressed in nineteenth-century fiction. The second chapter covers the "pulp" fiction of the mid-twentieth century. The rest of the book surveys the post-1970 explosion in vampire fiction, broadly dividing alien vampire characters into two classes, depending on their involvement with or separation from humanity. These characters range along a continuum of likeness and difference, intimacy and detachment, foregrounding a variety of issues generated by the interaction between "our kind" and the Other.

Chapter 1

Precursors:
Aliens Literal and Metaphorical
(Through the 1920s)

A case may be made for identifying Grendel as the first alien vampire in English literature. Described as a dweller in perpetual darkness, he drinks the blood of his victims before devouring them. Beowulf slays Grendel's mother by decapitation, one of the traditional methods of destroying a vampire. The epic constantly emphasizes Grendel's status as an outcast, a descendant of Cain yet no longer human. An apt example of the "superstitious doubting of another's humanity", the *Beowulf* poet frames Grendel, despite his derivation from Adam's lineage, as irredeemably cut off from the network of kinship and fealty central to the world of the poem.

In view of this vivid portrait of an inhuman, bloodthirsty monster whose plight as despised Other is sometimes pitiable as well as horrible, we might wonder why the vampire as literal alien--a natural but nonhuman sentient creature--appears seldom in novels and short stories before the twentieth century and not at all before the mid- to late nineteenth. When the vampire first appears by that name in English fiction, he is, as Nina Auerbach observes, domestic rather than foreign. Count Dracula, at the end of the nineteenth century, is "alien"--although metaphorically rather than literally--in a sense that Lord Ruthven and Sir Francis Varney are not. Both of these characters are English and, along with the homoerotic friendship between Laura and Carmilla in J. Sheridan LeFanu's story, support Auerbach's argument that affinity, not predation, dominates early to mid-nineteenth-century vampire fiction. She notes that vampires such as Lord Ruthven are not "snarling aliens...but singular friends", characterized not by "their difference from their human prey, but through their intimate intercourse with mortals" (13). She sees "Dracula's disjunction from earlier, friendlier vampires" as symbolized by his lack of a reflection, "his blankness, his impersonality" (63). Count Dracula's obsession with dominance rather than intimacy is illustrated by the pivotal scene in Chapter 21 of Stoker's novel. The Count's assault on Mina, forcing her to drink his blood, has been misread (in the Bloomian sense) over and over on film and in revisionist works such as Fred Saberhagen's *The Dracula Tape* (1975) as an act of erotic intimacy. I certainly do not deny the validity of a sexual reading on a symbolic level. On the surface of Stoker's text, however, Dracula claims to be motivated by a hunger for power and vengeance, not sexual fulfillment; he force-feeds his blood to Mina in order to use her against the men who hunt him. Auerbach reads the novel as dominated by "hierarchies, erecting barriers hitherto foreign to vampire literature," for example, "between male and female, antiquity and newness, class and class, England and non-England"

(66). *Dracula* and its successors exhibit "a new fear: fear of the hated unknown" (66-67).

Count Dracula behaves as a foreign invader, a potential conqueror, a role implicit in the warlike past of which he boasts to Jonathan Harker in Chapter 3. When Jonathan finds Dracula dormant in his coffin, he perceives the vampire as an invader, "the being I was helping to transfer to London, where...he might, amongst its teeming millions...create a new and ever-widening circle of semi-demons to batten on the helpless" (67). Ken Gelder notes, "Vampirism is colonisation--or rather, from the British perspective, *reverse* colonisation" (12, Gelder's emphasis). As Rhys Garnett observes, however, the vampire embodies a still more comprehensive threat than the invasion of England from the East: "Humanity at large is in danger of colonisation by the mutant sub-species of which Dracula is the source and centre" (36). Dracula, early in his acquaintance with Jonathan, lays stress upon his own non-Englishness, linking it to his drive for domination. In his own land, he says, "the common people know me, and I am master. But a stranger in a strange land, he is no one" (28). His desire to retain mastery by concealing his foreign origin motivates him to ask Jonathan's help in polishing his English. In the same conversation he warns his guest, "We are in Transylvania; and Transylvania is not England. Our ways are not your ways, and there shall be to you many strange things" (29). The motif of Otherness foregrounded in the novel's opening paragraph, when Jonathan ruminates on "leaving the West and entering the East" (1), remains a pervasive theme throughout. At one point Van Helsing speaks of Dracula as not merely a minion of Satan but as potentially "the father or furtherer of a new order of beings, whose road must lead through Death, not Life" (360)--in other words, a new species evolved from humanity through a sort of diabolical mutation, the "circle of semi-demons" feared by Jonathan.

According to Gelder, *Dracula* belongs to a complex of "horror fantasies in which self-identities are invaded by and absorbed into the Other" (12). This alienation is exemplified in the demonizing of Lucy. After her transformation into a vampire, Dr. Seward, formerly devoted to her, glories in the prospect of her destruction and calls her "the foul Thing which had taken Lucy's shape without her soul" (260). He regards her as no longer part of the human species. The vampire's alien status constitutes both threat and attraction, as implied in John Allan Stevenson's analysis of sexuality in *Dracula*. Contrary to earlier critics who interpret the novel in terms of symbolic incest, Stevenson suggests that Count Dracula's "sexual threat" consists of "a sin we can term excessive exogamy" (139). Dracula cannot perform the vampiric version of sexual intercourse--sucking blood--with his own kind, but must seduce yet-untransformed women. Guilty of "interracial sexual competition" (139), the vampire is dangerous because he corrupts and steals "our" women, releasing their sexuality in demonic modes, rather than within the domesticating bounds of monogamy. With his "omnivorous appetite for difference, for novelty" (139), Count Dracula gives his victims erotic experiences the male heroes of the novel cannot match. Concerning the scene in which the Count forces Mina to drink from him, Stevenson remarks, "What is going on? Fellatio? Lactation? It seems the vampire is sexually capable of everything" (146).

Rosemary Jackson also sees ambivalence toward Dracula's sexual prowess as central to the novel. In her view, Stoker objectifies forbidden desires in the vampires in order to assert society's conservative values by exterminating the vampires and, with them, subversive drives that threaten to break out. Garnett, similarly, reads the novel as a process of projecting "imperial and sexual guilt and fear" onto "primarily...non-English, non-bourgeois and (therefore) non-human figures, 'archetypes of the Other'" (31) and thereby exorcising these negative emotions. Through the staking of Dracula's three "wives" and Lucy, according to Jackson, "Stoker reinforces social, class, racial, and sexual prejudices" (121) and simultaneously "reasserts a prohibition on exogamy" (119). Like Stevenson, she sees the vampire in *Dracula* as an alien whose sexuality exerts such a powerful allure that it must be suppressed at all costs. Unlike Stoker's original audience, the late twentieth-century reader, far from identifying with the drive to suppress the vampire's "exogamy" and erotic omnicompetence, is apt to view these traits in a positive light.

Count Dracula and his "brides" invite ambivalent readings because, as formerly human creatures, they transgress and render permeable the boundary between human and nonhuman. The few literally alien vampires discoverable in nineteenth-century fiction stand firmly on the nonhuman side of the border. As we move from the metaphorically alien Dracula to the natural but nonhuman creatures discussed in the remainder of this chapter, we find that vampires who have never been human are easier to treat as wholly Other, fit only to be feared or destroyed. The invisible monster in Fitz-James O'Brien's mid-century tale "What Was It?: A Mystery" (1859) has much in common, like Grendel, with the "ogres" mentioned by Lewis in "Unreal Estates". Grendel, indeed, as an outcast descendant of Cain, possesses a stronger claim to humanity than O'Brien's creature. Editor Jessica Amanda Salmonson, in her background note on "What Was It?", calls this tale "likely the most influential single story aside from those of Poe in the development of modern supernatural horror" (155) and credits it with influencing Guy de Maupassant's "The Horla" (to be discussed below). While O'Brien's monster does not display the obviously vampiric traits found in Maupassant's Horla, O'Brien's nameless entity does bite its victims, with the apparent goal of either drinking blood or devouring flesh, like the cannibalistic trolls and ogres of folk tradition.

O'Brien's narrator, Harry, prides himself on his role as objective, scientific observer, yet the terms he applies to the creature vacillate between the scientific and the superstitious. He begins his narrative by remarking that the boarding house in which he lives "has enjoyed...the reputation of being haunted" (83). He summarizes the recent history of the house, along with the death of the former owner, which proves to be a red herring, unconnected to the "haunting". The new inhabitants expect the visit of a ghost with pleasurable anticipation, as implied by the word "enjoyed". Although previous tenants have reported phenomena suggestive of what we would now call poltergeist activity, Harry and his friends are disappointed by the absence of supernatural manifestations. When the invisible creature drops onto Harry's chest as he lies in bed, its solidity contradicts the expectations raised by the conventional "haunted house" setting. Further ambiguity concerning the assailant's status arises from Harry's habit of smoking opium with his friend Dr. Hammond--a habit "regulated with scientific accuracy" (85), an ironic claim in view of Harry's dismissal of the butler's testimony about a possible preternatural event on the grounds of the butler's habitual drunkenness. When Dr. Hammond suggests that the invisible attacker is no more than an opium dream, Harry seems to recognize no parallel between his own drug habit and the butler's alcoholism. The doctor's own observations, however, along with those of the other boarders, remove any doubt as to the creature's physical reality.

On an emotional level, though, the ambivalence of the observers' reaction, wavering between a scientific and a superstitious response, remains unresolved. Attacked in darkness, Harry initially assumes his assailant to be human, although naked, uncontrollably violent, and unusually strong. After restraining the creature and discovering its invisibility, he still wavers in his assessment of its nature. It has a humanoid shape, a roughly human (though hairless) head and face, "warm breath", and "skin...smooth, just like my own" (89). Harry rejects this implication of kinship, however, referring to the unknown being as a "creature", a "terrible Enigma", and a "something or other" (89). Dr. Hammond, after helping him bind the captive more securely, strives to comfort him by directing his thoughts into objective rather than emotional channels, assuring him that the creature's existence, though "awful", is "not unaccountable" (91). Hammond, in the role of scientist, draws an analogy with pure, completely transparent glass. In answer to the objection that the complexity of a living organism precludes the transparency of glass, Hammond cites the reported spiritualist phenomenon of "warm, fleshly", but invisible hands sometimes felt by participants in seances (92). Thus he attempts to assimilate data usually considered supernatural into the scientific world-view. But when Harry presses him for an opinion on the entity's nature, Hammond has none to offer, only resolving that, as a proper scientist, he will "thoroughly investigate it" (92).

Yet the doctor and Harry have already prejudged their captive on one point; they implicitly deny it human status. Just as Dr. Seward dehumanizes the resurrected Lucy as a "Thing", O'Brien's creature is always called "it", never "he" (in fact, its sex remains indeterminate). They spend little time questioning the propriety of keeping it tied up on Harry's bed, although they perceive "something truly terrible" in its "terrible writhings and agonized struggles for liberty", the repetition of the emotive word "terrible" underscoring the difficulty of maintaining their investigative detachment (92). The only proposed alternative to releasing the monster is killing it. Unlike the scientists they profess to be, the two investigators make no attempt to turn it over to outside researchers. Instead, the inhabitants of the house are sworn to secrecy. The only outsiders exposed to the creature are "Dr. X", who sedates it for the purpose of making a plaster cast of its form, and the artisan who sets the plaster. No one devises a scheme for attempting to communicate with it. They treat it like a subhuman animal, an assessment of its nature supported by its violent attack on Harry. The administration of chloroform, in order to prepare the cast, suggests the activity of vivisectionists.

Once the plaster cast renders the creature's appearance visible, the observers react emotionally rather than objectively. The entity is "shaped like a man", although only four feet tall, very muscular, and "[d]istorted, uncouth, and horrible" (93). Since the only pronoun applied to the monster remains "it", we cannot tell whether the narrator uses "man" in the sense of "male" or simply "human being", though the emphasis on "muscular development" (93) throws weight toward the former reading. Harry's description gives no hint of the precise nature of the "distortion" he perceives, nor does he describe the being's face. Instead of translating his reaction into objective terms, he compares its "hideousness" (93) to the work of artists such as Gustave Dore. At last he resorts to terms drawn from superstition, characterizing the creature as a "ghoul" that appears "capable of feeding on human flesh" (93). His ostensible scientific objectivity simply collapses. All the other boarders flee the house, leaving the creature to Harry and Dr. Hammond, who lapse into bewildered inaction. Unwilling "that such an awful being should be let loose upon the world", nevertheless they cannot bring themselves to destroy "this horrible semblance of a human being" (93). The word "semblance" foregrounds their denial of the creature's possible human status. After about a fortnight the entity starves to death. When Harry says, "Every thing in the way of nutriment that we could think of was placed before it, but was never touched" (93), he sounds as if he is trying to feed a dangerous pet rather than conducting a scientific experiment. (The monster's failure to eat any of the foods offered, by the way, supports the conjecture that its usual "nutriment" is human flesh and blood.) Harry feels "miserable" during the "terrible life-struggle" and finds the captive's suffering "pitiful" (93). These impotent emotions, however, do not bridge the gulf between his own humanity and the monster's perceived subhumanity. Like Grendel and Lucy, it is demonized, excluded from humankind. To the end, Harry names it "the Horror" and "the Mystery" (93). The story's subtitle, "A Mystery", seems not only to denote the tale's generic category but also to answer the question posed by the title: "What Was It?"

The narrator of Maupassant's "The Horla" (1886) discovers more about the nature of his tormentor--or believes he does--than do O'Brien's investigators. I pass over the question of whether Maupassant's story recounts a "real" experience or a delusion spawned by the narrator's mind, although I believe the narrative's internal evidence weights the reading in the direction of objective reality. For example, the coachman's symptoms and the servants' complaints of poltergeistlike incidents provide independent corroboration of occult phenomena. While the narrator does appear insane by the end of the story, it remains unresolved whether the Horla drives him mad or his madness generates the delusion of the Horla. Instead of pursuing this argument, I wish to discuss the nature of the eponymous alien, whether or not a "real" entity.

One initially striking difference from O'Brien's creature is that the Horla is framed as unequivocally superhuman rather than subhuman. Whereas O'Brien's characters, after the initial attack, keep the invisible monster as a helpless captive, Maupassant's narrator feels himself the prisoner and thrall of his monster. His descent into misery begins with the story's second journal entry, in contrast to the euphoric tone of the first entry, in which he mentions the arrival of the Brazilian ship that he later conjectures to have brought the Horla to Europe. Like O'Brien's narrator, Maupassant's unnamed journal-writer tries to apply rational analysis to his experience. He speculates on "the source of these mysterious influences which convert our happiness into depression and our confidence into anxiety," attributing emotional fluctuations to environmental conditions that affect the senses and bodily functions and, through them, the "soul" (136). Throughout the story, he vacillates between faith in medical explanations of his malaise and belief in a preternatural force preying upon him. Whenever he leaves his house, health and apparent rationality return; at home, he once again falls ill and, depending upon his mood, either recognizes the Horla's presence or fears madness. By the story's conclusion, he abandons the "madness" theory and fully accepts the entity's existence.

Though apparently a psychic as well as a physical predator, the Horla manifests itself in a material form reminiscent of O'Brien's creature. The first inkling of the predator's presence comes in the shape of a nocturnal attack similar to Harry's experience. Maupassant's diarist reports sensations of "someone creeping towards me--someone who looks at me, passes his hands over me, climbs up on to the bed, kneels on my chest, grasps my throat with both hands, and squeezes" (138). The imagery of sexual violation distinguishes this incident from O'Brien's analogous scene, but so does the fact that from the beginning the Horla is characterized as "someone", not "something", and "he", not "it". Personified, the Horla even displays a preference among victims; he preys upon the coachman only when the narrator is away from home. The creature demonstrates his materiality not only by physical attacks, "squatting" on the narrator's chest, "drinking [his] life from between [his] lips" and "draining [his] vitality like a leech" (141), but also by drinking water and milk left at the bedside. In an attempt at rational investigation, the narrator performs an experiment to demonstrate that he himself is not consuming the liquid in a somnambulistic trance. In the process, he discovers the selectivity of the Horla's appetite; the intruder disdains wine, bread, and strawberries. (Maupassant may be alluding to the tradition, in some cultures, that vampires dry up cows by draining their milk.) Later he witnesses an invisible entity producing physical effects, such as plucking a rose and turning pages.

At the same time, the Horla also manifests itself as a psychic predator. It gains control (though apparently intermittent) over the actions of the narrator, who believes that his "mind has become the chattel and serf of some other being" (151). He regards himself as possessed by "an alien will...like a second soul, parasitic and tyrannical" (151), imagined as similar to the compulsion of hypnosis, as demonstrated by an experiment performed by a mesmerist upon the narrator's cousin. The narrator sees hypnosis as a "mysterious dominion over the human soul," imperfectly understood by human experimenters, but perfected as "the weapon of our future Lord and Master," the Horla (154). Human beings occupy the position of lower animals in relation to this entity; the narrator assumes the role of a dog attacking its master, "a rebellious wild beast about to disembowel its tamer" (153). The threatened annihilation of his will and personality are symbolized by the moment when he looks into a mirror and cannot see his own image, because the Horla's invisible body blots it out, an inversion of the familiar belief that a vampire casts no reflection.

Although, when the narrator discovers a newspaper account of a South American superstition that seems to confirm the existence of the Horla, he reads that the "tangible but not visible" beings who torment the natives are "a species of vampire" (153), he does not take refuge in the supernatural as an explanation of his ordeal. Instead, he strives to fit the Horla into an evolutionary model, as a being that "is to be man's successor upon earth" (152). Though he speculates about a possible extraterrestrial invasion, he ultimately settles upon a theory of the Horla as the next stage in the development of terrestrial life. "There are a certain number of species on this earth," he reminds himself. "Why should not another variation arise...?" (155). He attributes his inability to see the Horla to the limitations of human senses and the higher refinement of the Horla's body, "more perfect than ours", with "finer qualities...more cunningly contrived" (155). The human body, in contrast, "is an animal mechanism, subject to maladies, deformities, putrefaction" and thus "a mere embryo of a being that might develop into something intelligent and sublime" (155). After what he believes to be his failed attempt to kill the Horla, he speculates that the creature's "transparent, mysterious, ethereal body" enjoys immunity to "illness, wounds, infirmities, or premature destruction" (159). Unlike H. G. Wells, who portrays his Martian invaders as vulnerable to disease and therefore still a part of the ecological web, Maupassant's narrator visualizes a superhuman vampire who, although in some sense material, transcends material limitations, subject to no force but time itself. *The War of the Worlds* concludes with a fortuitous second chance for humanity; in "The Horla", humankind, subject to death at "any day, any hour, any minute, by any sort of accident," is portrayed as doomed to be superseded by "that Being...who can die on this account alone, that his time-limit has run out" (159). The narrator assimilates the supernatural into this evolutionary model with the theory that primitive humanity "felt the approach of its master" (152) and, in response, imagined such beings as "gnome, spirit, genie, fairy, or goblin" (154) to embody its formless terrors. Where O'Brien's narrative rationalizes its "ghost" into a subhuman, invisible creature, Maupassant's rationalizes its "vampire" into a similar entity conceived as invisible but superhuman.

"The Last of the Vampires" (1893), by Phil Robinson, with its mention of "connecting links" and "the evolution of man from reptile" (146), draws upon Darwinian theory to introduce a naturally evolved vampire that is solidly material and apparently subhuman. The frame narrator compiling the "facts" of the case, however, introduces several different perspectives on the discovery of "the skeleton of a creature with human legs and feet, a dog-like head and immense bat-like wings" (146). Sometimes called "the man-lizard of the Amazon" and sometimes described as "a winged man with a dog's head" (147), initially the creature resists unequivocal classification as either human or animal. Eventually part of the skeleton disappears from the museum where it is stored, leaving no tangible proof of its existence (as in the conclusion of *Dracula,* where Jonathan notes the destruction of almost all original documents that might support the truth of the narrative). The frame narrator explains the skeleton's origin in the tale of an ambitious professor's determination to capture the last of the "vampires" to whom the Zaporo Indians, a South American tribe, sacrifice their captives. The German professor behaves like a typical nineteenth-century European colonial expansionist, confident of his superiority over the superstitious natives. He guides his canoe along the river into the vampire's cave, wounds the creature, first with a spear thrust and later with a blow to the head, binds it, and travels downstream with his "trophy...the last of the Winged Reptiles" (151). The cave-dweller's cooperation with the tribe's sacrificial rites hints at possible intelligence, but the professor never raises this question.

On the contrary, he displays no doubt of the vampire's subhumanity. What he sees when he first flashes a light into the cave is "a beast with a head like a large grey dog" and "eyes...as large as a cow's" (150). It dislikes sunlight, feeds on the blood of mammals, and has huge, batlike wings and a long neck. The professor identifies it as a "great bat-reptile of a kind unknown to science" and "a living specimen of the so-called extinct flying lizards of the Flood" (150). In between fighting off the creature's initial attacks, he gloats over his captive. He reveals little or no concern for the advancement of science. Rather, he is "devoured by only one ambition--to keep it alive, to let Europe actually gaze upon the living, breathing survivor of the great Reptiles known to the human race before the days of Noah" (152). He cherishes this dream, not for the benefit of science, but for his own aggrandizement. In the midst of his endless journey down the river, ravaged by fever, he consoles himself, "But in

Germany I shall be famous. *In Germany with my Vampire!*" (153, Robinson's emphasis). To him the creature is not only a mere animal, "a hideous beast", a "winged kangaroo with a python's neck" (152), but his personal possession. He doses the vampire with his entire supply of quinine, leaving none for himself, not out of regard for its welfare, but to preserve the trophy on which his ambitions depend. His description of its feeding technique, enfolding the victim in its wings and inducing paralysis, does not reveal scientific detachment on his part. Rather, he says, "To see it eating is terrible," and dwells on the "horrible thought" of its attacking him while delirious from fever (152).

The professor's ambition to become "the foremost of travellers in European fame--the hero of my day" (151) leads to a self-destructive contradiction. He resolves that if he finds himself dying, he will destroy the creature rather than resign himself to losing it. Whereas a disinterested scientist might choose to release the vampire, to preserve the last living specimen of an endangered species, the professor chooses to kill it instead of risking someone else's usurping his imagined fame: "If we cannot go back to Germany alive, we will go together dead. I will throttle it with my two hands, and fix my teeth in its horrible neck" (153). He not only becomes dehumanized to the point of barehanded violence but, ironically, adopts vampirelike behavior. Later the mingled bones of the professor and the vampire, with part of each washed away by the river, are found and mistaken for the skeleton of a single creature. The disappearance of the specimen, mentioned at the beginning of the story, completes the obliteration of the professor's discovery. Not only does he fail either to win fame or to contribute to scientific knowledge, he loses his identity in a physical merging with his vampire captive. The boundary between animal and human dissolves, to the discredit of humanity.

Much twentieth-century vampire-as-alien fiction uses its science fiction framework to delineate sympathetic vampires who, to some extent, share human traits that may be regarded positively. *The War of the Worlds* (1898), like Robinson's story, draws human-alien analogies that are far from complimentary to either our own species or the invaders. Wells' novel, as noted above, also views its aliens from an evolutionary perspective. His Martians, although superhuman rather than subhuman, are, unlike the Horla, not invulnerable. Wells' narrator takes pains to rationalize their behavior as a natural consequence of their position at the top of the food chain, as well as an inevitable result of interspecies competition for living space. On the ground that "life is an incessant struggle for existence," the narrator concedes that the Martians are justified, from their own viewpoint, in leaving their barren world to invade ours. He observes that to the Martians we must appear "at least as alien and lowly as are the monkeys and lemurs to us"; we are "what they regard as inferior animals" (310). They boast "minds that are to our minds as ours are to those of the beasts that perish, intellects vast and cool and unsympathetic" (309). Yet the "natural selection of our kind" (444), although it has made *Homo sapiens* inferior to the Martians, ultimately works in our favor, since the sterility of Mars leaves the invaders vulnerable to the microorganisms that our evolutionary heritage enables us to resist.

The War of the Worlds shares the invasion motif with *Dracula*. "In both", as R. J. Dingley points out, "England is infiltrated by alien creatures of more-than-human power, and familiar locations...become the settings for nightmare events" (13). Both Dracula and Wells' Martians leave their barren, exhausted homes to conquer fertile new lands. According to Dingley, Dracula explicitly (as the Martians do implicitly) "endorses the right of conquest of superior races" (16), particularly in his proud recitation of the glories of his ancestors. The British readers of Wells and Stoker were accustomed to the role of the conqueror, not the conquered. Wells' narrator compares the Martians' invasion to the extinction of the bison and the dodo, as well as the fate of the

Tasmanians, who "in spite of their human likeness, were entirely swept out of existence in a war of extermination waged by European immigrants" (311). In relegating England's inhabitants to the inferior position of conquered aborigines, as Stanislaw Lem remarks, Wells "inflicted blow after blow upon the jingoistic pride of his contemporaries" (26). Wells' narrator, recalling the "infinite complacency" of his countrymen before the invasion, notes that if the people of Earth had entertained the possibility of extraterrestrial life at all, they "fancied that there might be other men on Mars, perhaps inferior to themselves, and ready to welcome a missionary enterprise" (309). The notion of superior aliens had never entered their minds.

Moreover, they expected "men"; instead, they confront creatures utterly inhuman. The narrator acknowledges his "sudden chill" at the first sight of tentacles and a "big greyish rounded bulk", where he "expected to see a man emerge" from the spaceship (321). His initial reaction to the Martians contains no hint of scientific objectivity: "Those who have never seen a living Martian can scarcely imagine the strange horror of its appearance" (321). Though he first interprets the creature by analogy to lower animals, with tentacles "resembling a little grey snake" and a body "the size, perhaps, of a bear" (321), he soon learns that *Homo sapiens,* rather, stands in the position of the inferior species. Toward the end of his ordeal he recognizes himself as "an animal among the animals", as helpless and ignorant as "a rabbit...returning to his burrow and suddenly confronted by the work of a dozen busy navvies digging the foundation of a house" (424). He draws a similar analogy when discussing the Martians' nutritional requirements, noting "how repulsive our carnivorous habits would seem to an intelligent rabbit" (408). John Huntington views the "repeated comparisons of the Martian destruction of humans to the European destruction of other animals and other humans" as an indictment of the social-Darwinian ethics used by Wells' contemporaries to justify their expansionist policies (84). According to Huntington, the novel implies that "humanity as a whole...has deserved the Martian invasion because as a whole humanity has lived by the evolutionary code itself" (84). In isolation, however, the passages comparing the Martians' survival-driven behavior to our own might be read, not as an ethical indictment, but as an implication that human ideals are no more than a culturally conditioned veneer over a substratum of purely Darwinian motives. In any case, either reading supports Anne B. Simpson's observation that "movement toward ethical enlightenment is posited but never realized" (145).

When the narrator alludes to the evolutionary justification for the Martians' behavior, he appears to be recommending scientific detachment rather than voicing condemnation. But his negative comments about the invaders take the form of emotive outbursts rather than philosophical arguments. His account of their blood consumption, for instance, illustrates his vacillation between the objective and the emotional. Although the blood-draining scene occupies only a small portion of the novel, it carries considerable subjective weight for the narrator. The repellent effect that the Martians' position in the food chain has upon him, undermining his attempt to view them with scientific objectivity, justifies calling them "vampires". The narrator makes a point of the fact that the Martians lack "all the complex apparatus of digestion" and do "not eat, much less digest" (408). Instead, he tells us that "blood obtained from a still living animal, in most cases from a human being, was run directly by means of a little pipette into the recipient canal" (408). In short, he describes a process of blood transfusion. Yet, although he has made it clear that Martians do not eat or digest, he repeatedly refers to their nutritional intake in terms of eating. He mentions a "peculiar hooting" that "invariably preceded feeding" (411) and later alludes to "the only occasion on which I actually saw the Martians feed" (416). Immediately after the dispassionate account quoted above, he acknowledges his "squeamish" reaction to the "horribly repulsive" act and admits, "I cannot bring myself to describe what I could not endure even to continue watching" (408). This imagery of bloodthirsty monsters links the aliens with the ogres and trolls of Grendel's line or, as Kathryn Hume puts it, "the classic, man-eating giant of fairy-tale" (287).

Upon his first glimpse of the Martians, the narrator connects them with mythical monsters, in his reference to "Gorgon groups of tentacles" (322). He views their overall appearance and behavior as "at once vital, intense, inhuman, crippled, and monstrous" (322). He sees their skin as "fungoid" and the "clumsy deliberation" of their movements as "unspeakably nasty" (322). Later he attempts to assess the aliens in objective terms, as shaped by their environment and the struggle for survival, but this assumed detachment is undercut by numerous expressions of revulsion. At one point he entertains speculation that "the Martians may be descended from beings not unlike ourselves, by a gradual development of brains and hands...at the expense of the rest of the body" (410). He cannot, however, contemplate this possibility without bias in favor of his own kind: "Without the body the brain would, of course, become a mere selfish intelligence" (410). Despite this speculation and the analogies between European imperialism and the Martian invasion, any suggestion of kinship between Martians and humankind remains transitory and undeveloped.

No communication between Martian and human, no mutual self-disclosure, occurs in Wells' novel. The two species remain in an "I-It" rather than "I-Thou" relationship. Lem objects that "[c]reatures so completely reduced down...to values that can only be termed instrumental, seem to me impossible, or at least unconvincing" (22). He maintains that "if it is to be regarded as a mind," the mind of an intelligent creature must exhibit disinterested curiosity about its environment, without which science cannot advance (22). Therefore, he suggests, "the Martians should at least be interested in humans, to the extent that we ourselves are interested in apparently useless crustaceans or vegetation" (22-23). The "purely aggressive functionalism" (23) to which Wells reduces his Martians leaves no room for any growth of understanding between them and humanity. Simpson interprets even the Martians' inferred telepathic ability as, not a potential mechanism for bridging the interspecies gulf, but another obstacle that renders "any possibility of communication between them and humanity...remote" (142), presumably on the ground that the Martians' telepathy functions only among themselves, not with other species. In the final analysis, they revert to Lichtenberg's "Unknown" that is "a menace because it is a menace."

Certainly the menace remains uppermost in the narrator's mind, as he reflects upon the invasion. The "broadening of men's views" (452) that he embraces as a beneficial aftereffect of the war has broadened the human perspective mainly in troubling directions. He cautions his audience "that we cannot regard this planet as being fenced in and a secure abiding-place for Man" (452). As Simpson notes, even after the Martians have been eliminated, the survivors do not find themselves in the familiar pre-invasion world they remember: "The Other, the alien, in appropriating our earth for his own, transforms it into a site where we in turn feel Other, alien" (144). Although Wells' narrator alludes to hypothetical future "unseen good or evil that may come upon us suddenly out of space", it is the "unavoidable apprehension" with which we must now regard the night sky that dominates his thoughts (452). Unlike *Dracula*, in which, as Dingley says, "Western humanity triumphs over the outsider", *The War of the Worlds* allows the human race to survive the alien invasion only as a result of a biological accident (19). Wells, according to Dingley, "seeks to affront the complacency of his readers", while Stoker "reinforces" it (22). Wells seems to imply that evolutionary pressures must inevitably render hostile any contact between alien species and that the superior will inevitably seek to destroy or enslave the inferior.

Algernon Blackwood's "The Willows" (1907) introduces a predatory alien intelligence less akin to humanity than the Martians and more indifferent than the Horla. The narrator and his companion, the Swede, isolated on an island in the Danube, find themselves threatened by unseen forces. They escape after discovering the body of an apparently drowned man, whom they identify as the victim the predatory intelligence has claimed in their place. The narrator first views the willows themselves as the threat; later he and the Swede speculate about "the spirits of the elements" and "the old gods" (41). They finally decide that they are dealing with neither of these "comprehensible entities", which "have relations with men, depending upon them for worship or sacrifice" (41). Instead, the strange humming sound that pervades the air and the funnel-shaped indentations in the sand are produced by beings that "have absolutely nothing to do with mankind" (41). The two characters, by "mere chance", have blundered into an area where "their space happens just at this spot to touch our own" (41). The eponymous willows are only "symbols of the forces that are against us" (42). This phenomenon prefigures H. P. Lovecraft's extradimensional entities, not so much hostile to humanity as indifferent.

According to the Swede, human "thoughts make spirals in their world", and the potential victims' "only hope lies in ignoring them, in order that they may ignore us" (42). As inhuman and awe-inspiring as the Horla, these entities are even less material and not at all interested in conquering the human species. Wherever "the veil between has worn thin" (40), the hazard exists that the aliens may become aware of human individuals and prey upon them almost at random. What these predators want from their prey remains unclear, but the text hints at a vampiric draining of the soul. The Swede warns the narrator that discovery by the entities would mean a fate worse than death: "Death... means either annihilation or release from the limitations of the senses, but it involves no change of character. *You* don't suddenly alter just because the body's gone" (40). Absorption by the aliens, on the other hand, "means a radical alteration, a complete change, a horrible loss of oneself by substitution" (40). Symptoms of their attack include the humming noise, the sound of "countless little footsteps", the sense of "a sort of inner suffocation" (42), as well as a glimpse of a hazy shape "coiling upon itself like smoke" that resembles "neither a human figure nor an animal," yet "as large as several animals grouped together" (45). After the Swede becomes delirious and attempts suicide, the preternatural phenomena subside, and the two men find the body of what they take to be "the victim that made [their] escape possible" (50). The indentations in the dead man's flesh--"Their awful mark!" (52)--suggest the stigmata of a vampire's feeding. Invading with no design of conquest, feeding with no selectivity as to prey, Blackwood's aliens stand at a further distance from humanity than any others we have examined. They embody the wholly Other, with which no communication is possible.

The monster in E. F. Benson's "Negotium Perambulans" (1923) shares with Blackwood's entities inhuman Otherness and a certain randomness in choice of victims; Benson's creature, though, is more material, more fixed in shape, and perhaps subhuman rather than superhuman. Like the narrators of "What Was It?", "The Horla", and "The Willows", the victims in "Negotium Perambulans" apparently fall prey to attack simply by being in the wrong place. (The journal-writer in "The Horla" conjectures that the entity chooses to lair in his house only because of the similarity between the white building and the white ship from which it leaped to shore.) The men slain by Benson's creature all inhabit a house whose original owner built it of materials taken from a church he destroyed, erecting his house on the same site, "keeping, in a very ecstasy of wickedness, the altar, and on this he dined and played dice afterwards" (230). This impious man's servants find him dying "with the blood streaming from his throat" and "withered to a bag o' skin, for the critter had drained all the blood from him" (230). In the present day, a Mr. Dooliss rebuilds the house and lives in it despite the warnings of the village clergyman, the narrator's uncle. In the vicar's eyes, Mr. Dooliss, as a habitual drunkard, risks damnation as well as the creature's vengeance. After breaking into the church and attempting to destroy the panel depicting the creature, Mr. Dooliss, too, is found dead, "skin and bones as if every drop of blood had been sucked out of him" (234). The last victim described in the tale, still another tenant of the accursed house, is a painter, John Evans, whose "inexplicably hellish" (237) style marks him as a fit target for monster's vengeance.

The vicar preaches that divine wrath, not an accident of location, accounts for the deaths of the creature's victims. The panel in the church depicts "the figure of a robed priest holding up a cross, with which he faced a terrible creature like a gigantic slug" (229). According to the vicar, the picture represents "some evil agency... of almost infinite malignity and power," identified with "the pestilence that walketh in darkness" from the ninety-first Psalm (229). Yet he also characterizes the "Thing, the Creature, the Business that trafficked in the outer Darkness" as "a minister of God's wrath on the unrighteous" (229), a role that seems to contradict the demonic nature he assigns to it. His wife, the narrator's Aunt Hester, loyally maintains this theory after the vicar's death; she reminds the narrator, "God has His instruments of vengeance on those who bring wickedness into places that have been holy" (234).

Other details in the story, however, undercut the assumption that the Thing is either a demon or an instrument of God. After Mr. Dooliss smashes the panel in the church, it mysteriously returns to its undamaged state. Aunt

Hester confesses uncertainty as to "whether the power of God had mended it or some other power" (234). Although the legend of the original house-builder's fate refers to "some huge black shadow" (230), other descriptions of the Thing make it sound concretely material and more animal than demonic, much less spiritual. The narrator speculates about "powers and presences" hidden in nature, "dwellers in the innermost, grafted into the eternal life of the world", as well as "dark secrets" from the same realm, among which belonged the Thing "of deadly malignity" (236). When he actually sees the creature, though, its appearance does not suggest the elemental force hinted at by this passage. He sees the painter, Evans, attacked by a thing "like some gigantic caterpillar", which emits "stale phosphorescent light" and "an odour of corruption and decay, as from slime that has long lain below water" (238). Described as "hairless, and slug-like in shape and in texture", and "like a snake about to strike", the creature has a subhuman character emphasized by its headlessness and its "orifice of puckered skin which opened and shut and slavered at the edges" (238). This blatantly genital imagery, combining phallic and vaginal characteristics, underscores both the narrator's revulsion and the creature's bestial nature. The "gurglings and sucking noises" (239) of its feeding further reinforce the impression of animal appetite. The only ambiguity the narrator perceives arises from the difficulty of grasping the Thing's body; although he comes into contact with "something material", he finds his hands sinking into it "as in thick mud", as if "wrestling with a nightmare" (238). Nevertheless, his observations lean toward a "material" rather than spiritual conclusion about the Thing's nature.

Before his death, the painter Evans reveals the principle behind the "awful malignity" of his art, the Darwinian recognition of "much in common between a cat and a fuchsia-bush" (237). His remark, "Everything came out of the slime of the pit, and it's all going back there" (237), foreshadows the slimy "odour of corruption and decay" emitted by the creature and lends weight to a classification of it as a beast driven by hunger rather than a malignant elemental or an instrument of divine wrath. Like Blackwood's extradimensional entities, Benson's Thing, although apparently subhuman rather than superhuman, embodies Otherness and a disinterested, appetite-driven behavior that precludes any communication between predator and prey.

Images of distance and hostility dominate the nineteenth-century and early twentieth-century vampire-as-alien fiction we have discussed. Evolutionary parallels between alien and human are sometimes offered, and Darwinian pressures are invoked to explain the behavior of both. These parallels, however, do not produce a sense of kinship, much less compromise and mutually beneficial exchange, between human and nonhuman. Authors consistently assume that whenever the struggle for survival forces our species and another into contact, hostility will result, and the stronger will attempt to destroy or absorb the weaker. Potential for likeness may exist, but difference, conflict, and alienation always prevail. As we shall see, the pulp fiction of the mid-twentieth century introduces the possibility of mutual self-disclosure and, occasionally, symbiotic exchange between vampire and human.

Chapter 2

Vampires Among Us:
Twentieth-Century Pulp Fiction
(1930-1970)

The earliest vampiric aliens found in the pulp fiction of the late 1920s and beyond continue to portray the Other as a threat, separated from humanity by a nearly impassable gulf. Not until mid-century do "good" alien vampires begin to play a prominent role in science fiction and fantasy. For example, A. E. Van Vogt's "Asylum" (1942) and "Proxy Intelligence" (1968) feature extraterrestrial invaders who prey upon both the blood and the psychic energy of human victims (and, incidentally, exert an influence upon Colin Wilson's later, more ambiguous novel of vampiric invasion, *The Space Vampires* [1976]).

H. P. Lovecraft's extradimensional invaders, indifferent to the organic life of our planet, appear, in Dirk Mosig's words, "to be inimical to man, in the same way that man would appear to be inimical to ants, should these get in his way" (107). They show a clear kinship with the entities lurking behind the facade of the natural world in Blackwood's "The Willows". As Stephen Dziemianowicz remarks, Blackwood's aliens regard humanity with "the same sense of cosmic indifference that informs so much of Lovecraft's horror fiction" (34). Lovecraft's extradimensional beings prey on humanity in various ways. Only in a few stories, however, notably "The Dunwich Horror" (1929), do they behave in an explicitly vampiric fashion.

Lovecraft's Great Old Ones, unlike their predecessors in "The Willows", sometimes condescend to interact with their human thralls, either in dreams or in cultic rituals. In "The Dunwich Horror", Lavinia Whateley, impregnated by Yog-Sothoth, gives birth to twins, a superficially human boy, Wilbur, and an invisible being that grows to gigantic size, suggestive of the Horla on a grander scale. Until his death and consequent unmasking Wilbur, although grotesquely inhuman below the waist, passes as a member of the community, albeit physically and socially peculiar. Only with the disintegration of his corpse does it become apparent that "the really human element in Wilbur Whateley must have been very small" (112). There is no suggestion that Wilbur engages in vampiric predation. His "twin brother" who "looked more like the father than he did" (133) lives upon the blood of cattle until Wilbur's death allows his escape from the barn in which he has been confined for most of his life. He then embarks on a rampage of destruction through the countryside. Unlike Blackwood's entities or the Horla, Wilbur's brother is half-human and displays the mark of that heritage when Dr. Armitage, an authority on the occult, momentarily renders him visible. Witnesses see an "octopus, centipede, spidery kind o' thing", with "a half-shaped man's face on top of it, an' it looked like

Wizard Whateley [Wilbur's grandfather], only it was yards an' yards acrost" (132). The creature proves human enough to appeal to Yog-Sothoth, in English, as "Father" the instant before his destruction (131). Despite this momentary touch of pathos, however, no one within the story questions the necessity for that destruction. What Richard E. Dansky labels the "territorial transgression" between the proper human and nonhuman "spheres of influence" is always presented as negative in Lovecraft's fiction (5). "The Dunwich Horror", in particular, according to Dansky, illustrates the principle that "[w]hat belongs Outside should stay Outside," and the "attempted crossbreeding (literally) of the two spheres" leads inevitably to destruction (5). Throughout the narrative, Wilbur is systematically distanced from humanity, first by his preternaturally rapid growth, then by the deaths of his mother and grandfather, and finally by the revelation, in death, of his physical abnormalities, to which the other characters respond with horror rather than pity. When his corpse dissolves, as noted above, rather like that of a classic literary or cinematic vampire, the stage is set for disregarding any "really human element" that might elicit compassion for the monstrous brother.

Lovecraft's only more or less traditional vampire tale, "The Shunned House" (1937), deals with a different kind of "territorial transgression" between human and nonhuman spheres. The Harris house in Providence, site of mysterious outbreaks of illness, madness, and death, at first appears a conventional haunted or cursed abode. Later the dwelling's evil force, located in the "fungous and malodorous cellar", is identified as a vampire, defined in supernatural terms as "the dead who retain their bodily form and live on the blood or breath of the living" (121). Research into historical records reveals an abandoned graveyard beneath the house, belonging to the Roulet family, a clan rumored to practice witchcraft and lycanthropy. Only the narrator's scientifically oriented investigation, with the help of his uncle, a medical doctor, probes behind the superstitions to uncover the inhuman dimensions of the "haunting". The narrator denies literal belief in vampires and werewolves. Instead, he admits "the possibility of certain unfamiliar and unclassified modifications of vital force and attenuated matter; existing very infrequently in three-dimensional space because of its more intimate connection with other spatial units, yet close enough to the boundary of our own to furnish us occasional manifestations" (128). The reanimated and radically transformed corpse of Paul Roulet exists in a liminal state between human and inhuman, mundane and alien. The Roulet family's "abnormal affinity for outer circles of entity--dark spheres which for normal folk hold only repulsion and terror" (128) opens the way for this transgression of boundaries. Thus human evil collaborates in the invasion of the Other from outside, as in "The Dunwich Horror". The alien entity in "The Shunned House", however, does not literally crossbreed with its human hosts, but rather interpenetrates and transmutes the late Paul Roulet, enabling "certain kinetic patterns...which obscurely survived" in the dead man's brain "to function in some multiple-dimensioned space along the original lines of force determined by a frantic hatred of the encroaching community" (128-129). (This plot device, a nonhuman entity's transformation of a human host with the host's mind used as a template, reappears in the novels *Sabella* and *Sunglasses After Dark*, discussed in the next chapter.) The narrator defines this entity as "an alien nucleus of substance or energy" fed by "subtractions from the life-force or bodily tissues of other and more palpably living things" (129). With these three-dimensional hosts "it sometimes completely merges itself" (129). Since the Roulets have apparently invited this merging, they are no more innocent than the alien invader. Whether "actively hostile" or driven "by blind motives of self-preservation", in the eyes of Lovecraft's narrator this kind of entity is a "monster" and "of necessity...an anomaly and an intruder", whose destruction is obligatory (129).

The explicitly vampiric traits of the beings spawned by the Lovecraft mythos are developed more fully by some of Lovecraft's disciples, such as Robert Bloch in "The Shambler from the Stars" (1935) and Frank Belknap Long in *The Horror from the Hills* (1931). Bloch's story features the killing of a character based on Lovecraft himself (with the latter's permission) by a Horla-like creature that visibly drains the victim's blood into its otherwise invisible form. Invoked by chance, through the "Lovecraft" character's arrogance in reading aloud an incantation from the ancient, forbidden volume that constitutes a standard feature of such stories, the creature summoned "from beyond the stars" (30) has no apparent motive besides ravenous hunger. The narrator sees his friend's "sagging body, dangling in midair, bent backward...as blood spurted from the torn neck" (31). Gorged with the victim's drained blood, the entity becomes visible as "an immensity of pulsing, moving jelly; a scarlet blob with myriad tentacular trunks" (32). A lighthearted pulp-horror tale, "Shambler" entertains no speculations about communicating with the entity or seeking a *modus vivendi* with it; it appears no more comprehensible or sympathetic than the Horla, although cruder in its mode of attack. In the manner typical of Lovecraftian protagonists, Bloch's narrator avoids destruction by accident, not by any wit or strength of his own. Like the two men in "The Willows", he survives because another victim sates the monster's appetite.

The deity Chaugnar Faugn in *The Horror from the Hills* has a more complicated relationship with its human worshippers and prey. Clark Ulman, the museum employee who brings back to America a vaguely elephantine idol, which proves to be Chaugnar Faugn himself (coming to life to attack his victims), nourishes the creature during the voyage with his own blood.

Consequently, like the victim of a traditional vampire, he becomes transformed into the predator's likeness, or, as he puts it, "the forbearance of Chaugnar Faugn has wrought an uncleanliness in my body's flesh, and blackened and shriveled my soul" (28). Just as Mina proclaims herself unclean after Dracula's attack, despite her status as victim, Ulman considers himself tainted. As soon as he has fulfilled his mission of delivering the deity to the museum, thereby loosing Chaugnar Faugn upon the outside world, he dies, and his body decays rapidly, like a vampire's or Wilbur Whateley's. (The rapid decomposition or outright disappearance of a cadaver often seems to symbolize the loss of humanity.) This blurring of identities between predator and prey, engendering pity for Ulman, only intensifies the characters' horrified revulsion toward Chaugnar Faugn.

Both Ulman and his colleague at the museum, Algernon Harris, begin by attempting to rationalize the deity in scientific terms. Ulman mistakes it for "some cave-lurking survivor from the age of reptiles--some atavistic and predatory abnormality that had experienced no necessity to advance on the course of evolution" (19). The Darwinian language is undercut by the emotive words "atavistic" and "abnormality"; ostensible scientific objectivity does not preclude horror. Later Ulman revises his view, though he refuses to acknowledge the "god" as omnipotent; instead, Chaugnar Faugn may be the natural product of "another evolutionary cycle" that "may have preceded the one which has culminated in us" (27). Harris, similarly, rejects Ulman's belief in Chaugnar Faugn's powers; stone, after all, cannot come to life. Harris attributes the changes in Ulman to hypnosis and plastic surgery. At last, though, it becomes clear that Chaugnar Faugn is a hyperdimensional entity, "a product of physical evolution on a plane incomprehensible to us" (98). Although "the spawn of remote worlds and unholy dimensions", it is "a creature and not a creator, a creature obeying inexorable laws" (98); thus, the protagonists can defeat it by sending it back through the time-space continuum to its point of origin. Like Wells' Martians, Chaugnar Faugn seeks contact with human beings only to enslave and prey upon them. Though it communicates with our kind through telepathy and dreams, there is no suggestion that such communication can lead to mutual disclosure between sentient minds; the human recipient remains the inferior. Therefore, as with a similar lesson in *The War of the Worlds*, the concluding sentence's message that humanity "is not isolated among the sentient beings of earth but is linked to all that moves in hyperdimensional continuity" (99) conveys no optimism but only a warning.

A more optimistic outcome concludes Eric Frank Russell's *Sinister Barrier* (1939), in which human ingenuity scores a decisive victory over a nonhuman species of psychic vampires. The novel begins with an outbreak of mysterious deaths and suicides among scientists, who leave cryptic messages suggestive of madness. Gradually the truth comes to light, that throughout the existence of *Homo sapiens,* humanity has been ruled and preyed upon by "luminescent spheres, about three feet in diameter, their surfaces alive, glowing, blue, but totally devoid of observable features" (104). These entities, "neither animal, mineral nor vegetable" but pure energy (105), given the name "Vitons", feed on violent emotions as well as certain kinds of electromagnetic energy. They use extrasensory perception and telepathy in lieu of material senses and modes of communication. Investigation uncovers a combination of drugs that allows ordinary people, not only those with paranormal perception, to see the Vitons. Revealed to the world, the Vitons strike back by provoking global disasters and warfare. Finally an electromagnetic wavelength capable of destroying them is discovered, and humanity annihilates its former masters.

The Vitons are even less individually personified than Wells' Martians. One character in *Sinister Barrier* characterizes the Vitons as "so utterly and completely alien that I cannot see how it will ever be possible for us to find a common basis that will permit some sort of understanding" (104). The emergence of humanity from its ignorant status as prey into clear-sighted knowledge constitutes the theme of the novel. Here, however, understanding is not, as in Lichtenberg's theory of Intimate Adventure, the key to interspecies cooperation; instead, understanding is the key to conquest and annihilation. Graham, Russell's protagonist, declares, "Ignorance may be bliss--but knowledge is a weapon" (95), and later he proclaims the need to "counterbalance the Vitons' enormous advantage in having an ages-old understanding of human beings, and gain an equally good comprehension of them. Know thine enemy!" (124).

The imagery of the novel dehumanizes both humanity and the superhuman predators. Russell's foreword reveals that he was inspired to write *Sinister Barrier* by Charles Fort's statement, "I think we're property" (2). Graham and his fellow investigators in the novel discover that the Vitons, whether invaders from another planet, creatures co-evolved with *Homo sapiens,* or possibly "true Terrestrials, while we are the descendants of animals which they've imported from other worlds in cosmic cattle-boats" (104), deliberately breed human beings for the emotional energy upon which the predators feed. The novel begins with a pair of metaphorical warnings: "Swift death awaits the first cow that leads a revolt against milking", and, "there's a swat waiting for the first bee that blats about pilfered honey" (5).

Other subhuman imagery includes a reference to a mental patient as "mutilated trash tossed aside by super-vivisectionists" (39); a contrast between the Vitons as "Lords of Terra" and "we, the sheep of their fields", kept under "their mastery as cold-bloodedly as we maintain ours over the animal world-- by shooting the opposition" (88-89); the suggestion that the Vitons perform "super-surgery on their cosmic cattle" for the same motives that lead some people to "teach seals to juggle with balls, teach parrots to curse, monkeys to smoke cigarettes and ride bicycles" (91) and medical students to "make stray cats disappear" and snatch "frogs that are later dissected" (92); and the characterization of a victim about to be drained as "a homoburger waiting the bite" (219). All terrestrial conflicts throughout history have been "grist for the Viton mill... unwitting feeders of other, unimaginable guts" (107). The human gene pool has been manipulated just as we shape crops such as potatoes; human beings are "emotional tubers... grown, stimulated, bred according to the ideas of those who do the surreptitious cultivating" (109).

This novel thus places the blame for the horrors of human history on an outside force. The Vitons constitute a science fiction analogue to Original Sin. One character warns his hearers, "Humanity will never know peace, never build a heaven upon earth while its collective soul bears this hideous burden, its collective mind is corrupted from birth" (110). Once freed from the tyranny of the psychic vampires, *Homo sapiens* is restored to the condition of freedom and self-determination that our species should have enjoyed all along. "We can emote for ourselves now, and not for others," Graham declares at the conclusion, for "in the truest sense we're now alone" (253). The text implies that in the absence of the Vitons, most human conflicts will cease, and our species will indeed "build a heaven upon earth" as well as, perhaps, welcome friendly extraterrestrials whom the Vitons have prevented from visiting our planet. Only the elimination of the corrupting outside force is required to initiate a terrestrial golden age.

From the 1930s on, fiction of the monstrous, wholly Other vampiric alien coexists alongside tales of more complex vampires, outwardly similar to ourselves, who span a range from menacing to harmless, with degrees of repulsion and attraction in between. The title character of C. L. Moore's "Shambleau" (1933) appears in humanoid, though not precisely human, shape, capable of enticing and seducing her prey, even capable of arousing sympathy. Ultimately, though, interplanetary adventurer Northwest Smith rejects her pathos and sexual allure as a snare, a temptation not unlike the corrupt voluptuousness of the resurrected Lucy in *Dracula*. Various critics have commented on the fear of female sexuality objectified in Stoker's treatment of his two heroines. Gail Griffin associates the characterization of Lucy with "the idea of woman as a subhuman, wholly animalistic creature" (142). Lucy "outrages the Victorian ideal" (143) with her expressed wish to marry all three men who propose to her, her outbursts of violence as a vampire, and her anti-maternal behavior of feeding on children. Griffin comments, "It has always been easy for a male-dominated culture to project the beast within upon the woman without, violently repressing her sexuality while just as violently encouraging it" (143). In Lucy's case, the repression consists of first trapping her in her tomb, then driving a stake into her body. In "Shambleau", the female vampire first appears as the target of a murderous mob of Martian citizens, whose spokesman tells Smith that they "never let those things live" (149).

Smith's perception of Shambleau undergoes several shifts. When he rescues her from the mob, he sees her in conventional terms as a victimized innocent, "a girl, and sweetly made and in danger"; he finds "something in her hopeless huddle at his feet that touched that chord of sympathy for the underdog that stirs in every Earthman" (148). A closer look at the girl reveals animal traits, eyes with "slit-like, feline pupils" and fingers "tipped with round claws that sheathed back into the flesh like a cat's" (151). He sees in her eyes "dark, animal wisdom in their depths--that look of the beast which sees more than man" (151). This perception of her as an animal drives him to reject her sexual advances. Alongside the "rising clamor of his blood", he feels "something within him shudder away"; he finds her touch "suddenly loathsome" and momentarily shares the "wild, feverish revulsion he had seen in the faces of the mob" (154). Nevertheless he continues to shelter her, insisting to himself that she is no more than "a pretty brown girl-creature from one of the many half-human races peopling the planets", simply an animal in quasi-human shape (155). His concept of her nature changes yet again when he beholds the "nest of blind, restless red worms... like naked entrails endowed with an unnatural aliveness" that she has in place of hair (159).

She preys upon him first in a dream, then in conscious paralysis, the serpentine tendrils on her head inducing a "warm softness... caressing the very roots of his soul with a terrible intimacy" and evoking a "rapture of revulsion, hateful, horrible--but still most foully sweet" (155). The oxymoron "foully sweet" epitomizes the queasy eroticism that pervades the story. The adjectival combination "wet and warm" (155 and passim) is applied to Shambleau over and over, emphasizing the salient marks of female sexuality in a context of repugnance and dehumanization. Smith's Venusian friend Yarol discovers Smith "slimy from the embrace of the crawling horror" (163). In the grasp of Shambleau's seduction, Smith experiences a "mingling of rapture and revulsion" in which "his body answered to the root-deep ecstasy, a foul and dreadful wooing from which his very soul shuddered away" (161). The creature's "slimy, ecstatic embrace" induces a "weakness... flooding that grew deeper after each succeeding wave of intense delight", a nearly explicit description of orgasm and ejaculation (162). Ernest Jones summarizes vampirism as a "nightly visit from a beautiful or frightful being, who first exhausts the sleeper with passionate embraces and then withdraws from him a vital fluid" and attributes the myth to the common experience of nocturnal emissions; in the symbolism of the unconscious, "blood is commonly an equivalent for semen" (119). "Shambleau" dramatizes this psychosexual subtext of the vampire myth by explicitly linking sexual ecstasy with the draining of life-force and, in terms reminiscent of the heroes' rejection of the transformed Lucy in *Dracula,* the violation of the soul. Shambleau's embrace inflicts a vampiric transformation upon Smith, making him appear "some creature beyond humanity--dead-alive" (163). Like the victim of a traditional vampire, he can be restored to himself only by the slaying of the monster, which Yarol accomplishes by employing a trick from the Medusa legend.

In the denouement Shambleau again becomes a "thing", referred to as "it" rather than "she". Yarol informs Smith that the creature's draining of life-force acts like a drug upon those men who survive the first embrace and thereafter "keep the thing with them all their lives--which isn't long--feeding it for that ghastly satisfaction" (166). Moore gives no hint that this exchange might stabilize into mutually beneficial symbiosis; Shambleau's seduction is framed as entirely negative, analogous to the deepest depravity of addiction. Her human appearance is probably an illusion to cloak the normal shape, a mass of writhing scarlet tentacles. Her serpentine appendages link her with the Gorgon and the Lamia; probably "an older race than man, spawned from ancient seed in times before ours, perhaps on planets that have gone to dust", her kind have spawned ancient myths on innumerable worlds (167). The only suggestion of potential communication with that species comes in Yarol's comment, "Wouldn't the records of that race of--of *things,* whatever they are, be worth reading! Records of other planets and other ages and all the beginnings of mankind!" (167). He instantly repudiates his own suggestion, however, relegating Shambleau's kind to the status of parasitic nomads without a culture. He compares them to "the Wandering Jew", connecting them with a traditional embodiment of otherness, an ethnic group often dehumanized by mainstream society (167). He denies that Shambleau's species possesses "any superhuman intelligence", comfortably categorizing them as animals who wield their "terrible hypnotic power" as "their means of getting food--just like a frog's long tongue or a carnivorous flower's odor" (167). Smith feels the tempting lure of his lost unity with Shambleau, the moment when he "saw things--and knew things--horrible, wild things... visited unbelievable places" (168). He rejects this memory as a temptation to be resisted, however, attributing the pleasure of the union to "some nucleus of utter evil in me--in everyone--that needs only the proper stimulus to get complete control" (168). The initial sympathy for Shambleau generated by her desperate plight in the opening scene is completely obliterated by this point. Rather than a quasi-human being who deserves humane treatment, she becomes "a mound like a mass of entrails" (162) that only apes human form, an alien of manageably animalistic nature and intelligence. Yarol forces Smith to promise, if he ever meets another Shambleau, to "draw your gun and burn it to hell the instant you realize what it is" (168). (Smith's reluctant, conditional promise represents the lingering taint upon his soul, not any moral qualm about killing an alien.) The Other, unmasked as radically unlike us, merits only preemptive destruction.

The boundary between "our kind" and the Other blurs in Jack Williamson's *Darker Than You Think* (1940). In this novel, after exploring decades of non-anthropomorphic aliens, we encounter naturally evolved vampires completely human in outward form. While the protagonist, Will Barbee, behaves as a werewolf for most of the novel, upon his "death" in Chapter 20 he rises as a vampire, with the implication that the transition to vampirism is a normal event in his species' life cycle. Despite the brief space in the narrative devoted to his experience as a vampire, this transformation is clearly depicted as the climactic, pivotal event in his personal odyssey. Moreover, *Homo lycanthropus* has grown to "like the taste of human blood, and they couldn't exist without it" (235), and like the undead of folklore, they require special treatment, after death, to prevent their rising from the grave.

Will's ancestral race is not a species wholly apart from humanity, but rather a co-evolved race that has lived secretly among *Homo sapiens* from prehistoric times. Williamson's novel proposes a sort of unified field theory of supernatural evil, attributing the darker side of human nature to crossbreeding with *Homo lycanthropus*. Psychic powers are rationalized in terms of manipulating energy fields through "direct mental control of probability" (93), a talent that even enables those with dominant lycanthropic genes to project their essences into astral form, in chosen animal shapes. Sunlight and silver disrupt the energy networks that the witch-men utilize. While all present-day human beings have some trace of lycanthropic heritage, a few possess powerful combinations of such traits. Will, unknown to himself, is an almost pure throwback, the "Child of Night" or dark Messiah awaited by the witch-folk. The almost equally powerful April Bell seduces him into using his powers, in what he believes to be dreams. In astral form he learns to take the shape of wolf, saber-toothed tiger, snake, and finally a dragonlike winged lizard. In these shapes he helps April kill off his friends, a group of investigators who have uncovered the truth about the witch-folk. Torn between the exhilaration of his new powers and the guilt of murder, Will evades the dilemma for as long as possible by convincing himself that his nocturnal escapades are no more than imagination.

Somewhat like Jack Finney's *The Body Snatchers* (1955), *Darker Than You Think*--the very title hinting at sinister secrets--embodies xenophobic wartime and (in Finney's case) Cold War paranoia, the vision of a world in which evil entities who look exactly like ordinary citizens prowl among us. As Richard Hofstadter explains in "The Paranoid Style in American Politics", this world-view postulates the existence of "a vast, insidious, preternaturally effective international conspiratorial network designed to perpetrate acts of the most fiendish character" (23). The archeologist Mondrick in Williamson's novel speaks of "a masked and secret enemy, a black clan that plots and waits unsuspected among true men--a hidden enemy, far more insidious than any of your modern fifth columns" (38). The foreigner and the racial Other, demonized to make their destruction a righteous crusade, stand apart from "true men". To these Others Mondrick attributes "the world's discord", "the daily news of crime", and the general "monstrosity of man"; he attributes "the malignant purpose behind misfortune" to *Homo lycanthropus* (38). This theory explains the "tragic division" in each individual, "the realization that your unconscious minds hold wells of black horror", as the result of lycanthropic taint (38). Not only does the enemy prowl unseen among us, it lurks within us as well, an appalling revelation that, paradoxically, offers comfort: The evil within us does not belong to us, but to the aliens who have tainted humanity with their corruption (just as, in *Sinister Barrier*, the strife that pervades terrestrial history arises from outside forces, not innate human weakness). As Ken Gelder points out, this kind of fiction focuses upon "revealing an underlying horror which is governing or manipulating events at the surface level", a horror "barely visible but nevertheless omnipresent" (125). Those few characters possessing the "paranoid consciousness" that enables them to see the hidden truth become the heroes, "measured against other characters who, by contrast, are not paranoid *enough*" (125, Gelder's emphasis).

In *Darker Than You Think,* despite the Darwinian rationale for the evolution of the witch-folk, Will's former friends make no pretense of viewing *Homo lycanthropus* with scientific dispassion. Instead, Will's colleague, Quain, strives to convert Will to the "paranoid consciousness". He explains how the "ice-bound nomads" destined to evolve into the witch-folk learned in prehistoric times to "prey on their more fortunate cousins [ordinary human beings]" (234). In the distant past their "dreadful powers" made them "the hunters and the enemies and the cruel masters of mankind", in a reign of "degrading, cannibalistic oppression" (235). Quain tops off this emotionally loaded anthropology lesson with the remark that the witch-folk served as models for "every ogre and demon and man-eating dragon of every folk tale" (235), like the Horla and Shambleau, casting their shadow through legend and superstition--or like Grendel, a cannibalistic outcast, humanoid but doomed never to be accepted as human. Quain expresses another paranoid fear, the dominant race's horror of miscegenation. Like other ethnic minorities, the witch-folk are imagined as "strangely passionate", possessed of hyperpotent sexuality (238). (This assumption about vampires becomes a dominant motif in more recent fiction.) Quain calls the hybridization of the two races an "ugly fact", which he attributes to "bestial ceremonies in which the daughters of men were forced to take part" (237). The analogy with Caucasian fear of rape by members of "inferior" races is inescapable. In Quain's view, the "alien inheritance" left from the "terrible past" constitutes a "black river of that monstrous blood... in the veins of Homo sapiens" (238).

By the time Will hears the full story of humanity's secret past, the presumption of *Homo lycanthropus'* unambiguous evil has already been undercut by the protagonist's discovery that he belongs to that "semi-human race" (233). He perceives his first astral transformation into lupine shape as the breaking of "painful bonds, that he had worn a whole lifetime", a liberation from his "slow, clumsy, insensitive bipedal body" (96). Aside from the moral quandary associated with killing, his nocturnal adventures with April Bell prove a positive experience. He exults in his new-found power, recognizing his human life as "a dim nightmare of bitter compromise and deadly frustration" (151). Capitalizing on his "desperate eagerness for escape", April tries to convince him that his "old, good friends"--his human friends--are his foes, "grasping every resource of science" to exterminate Will's own kind (151). In a mirror image of Quain's diatribe, she portrays her people as victims, not devils. Yet despite his pleasure in the "hot sweet taste" of blood, Will nevertheless feels "cold and ill" after slaughtering one of his former friends; though he views his physical body as a "narrow, ugly prison", he feels morally obligated to return to it (156). His final transformation, the death of his body and his release as a vampire, bestows complete liberation. April responds to his initial shock with, "You're a vampire now, and you might as well learn to like it" (280). And that is essentially what he does. His dilemma of conscience is not so much solved as simply forgotten in the ecstasy of attaining his full powers. He destroys Quain, not as a result of a considered ethical decision, but in pure self-preservation, casting his lot with his nonhuman heritage. The novel's denouement leaves the reader with a radically ambiguous view of the "good" and "evil" dichotomy between *Homo sapiens* and *Homo lycanthropus.*

The work of Ray Bradbury generally embodies a more benign view of the relationship between human and nonhuman. One exception is "The Man Upstairs" (1947), in which the boy protagonist saves his family and friends from an alien vampire of enigmatic nature but unambiguous menace. Eleven-year-old Douglas becomes suspicious of his grandparents' new boarder, Mr. Koberman, who stays out all night, sleeps all day, carries no silver coins, and eats with his own wooden cutlery instead of silverware. The story, like many of Bradbury's works, focuses on the fresh, imaginative world-view of childhood. Free of adult preconceptions, Douglas realizes the significance of Koberman's aversion to the multicolored panes of glass in one of the upstairs windows. Through the colored glass Douglas sees "worlds... All different" (217). By peering at the stranger through the glass, he can penetrate Koberman's human facade to perceive his inner alienness. Thus confirming his intuitive sense of Koberman's anomalous nature, Douglas, unlike the adults with their linear logic, realizes the stranger's connection with the mysterious recent deaths in town. Because of his fascination with his grandmother's chicken-butchering procedures, Douglas has no qualms about removing Koberman's peculiar internal organs. The strange man survives even after the dissection, until Douglas sews a cache of silver dimes into the body cavity. Though his grandfather thinks the boy should be taken on a trip to "forget this whole ghastly affair," Douglas replies, "I don't see anything bad. I don't feel bad" (223). Living in a different mental and perceptual world from his elders, he is, in a sense, as alien to them as Koberman is. Earlier, Grandpa cautions against being too quick "to call anything by a name", even "a hobgoblin or a vampire or a troll" (220). Rather than filing the sources of our fears into "categories with labels," we should recognize them as, "People who do things" (220). This open-minded attitude evaporates, however, when Douglas' surgery reveals Koberman's true nature. To the question, "What was Koberman? A vampire? A monster?" the coroner can reply only, "Something--not human," with which all the adults in the story agree (224).

More often, however, nonhuman vampires in Bradbury's fiction appeal to the reader's sympathy. His Elliott Family, introduced in "Homecoming" (1946), lives secretly and apart from human society, and, unlike Williamson's witch-folk, harmlessly. "Homecoming", one of several stories about the Family, centers upon the pathos of young Timothy's situation as the only ordinary child in a clan of vampires, shapeshifters, and witches. Bradbury reverses conventional concepts of "normal" and "abnormal" (foreshadowing numerous such inversions in more recent fiction), defining the "human" boy, rather than his night-haunting relatives, as a misfit. Timothy views himself as defective; gazing into his mirror, the only one in the house, he laments "the poor, inadequate teeth nature had given him" and yearns for "strong teeth, with incisors like steel spikes. Or strong hands, even, or a strong mind... But, no, he was the imperfect one, the sick one" (250). At the All-Hallows Eve gathering, his mother demonstrates her affectionate concern while explaining his diurnal habits and dislike for blood to visiting relatives: "He's my son, and he'll learn" (254). The pity of the adults and the sly teasing of Timothy's cousins and siblings contribute to a mirror-image reversal of a "normal" family worried and embarrassed by a "defective" child. His sister Cecy, a bedridden witch who travels with her mind, takes temporary possession of his body to allow him to drink blood and otherwise impress the guests at the party. She betrays him, though, callously using him to deliver a message to the visitors. Winged Uncle Einar comforts him with the assurance, "How much better things are for you. How rich. The world's dead for us... Life's best to those who live the least of it" (260). Through this experience, Timothy learns to embrace his limitations, makes up with Cecy (who once more helps him to participate in the festivities), and accepts his mother's vow, "We all love you. No matter how different you are, no matter if you leave us one day" (262). "Homecoming" is a rarity for its time, a non-humorous vampire story populated by an entirely inhuman cast of characters, with the "imperfect" boy serving as a stand-in for the "normal" human point of view.

Timothy's kindly uncle later appears in his own tale, "Uncle Einar" (1947). This creature with "beautiful silk-like wings...like sea-green sails" (192) abandons the night world to marry an ordinary mortal, Brunilla. They meet when, on the way back to Europe from the Homecoming, Einar collides with a high-tension wire. Brunilla accepts him, "startled", but, since "she had never been hurt in her life...she wasn't afraid of anything" (193). Instead of showing fear, she "stroked his large green membraned wings with careful envy" (194). With his "delicate night-perception" (194) destroyed by his electrocution, Einar can no longer fly in the dark. He now suffers, in fact, a handicap similar to Timothy's; he no longer shares the powers inherent in their family's genes. He cannot risk flying by day in a populated area, for fear of being "shot down" or "kept for a zoo" (194). He represents an early example of the persecuted "monster", like the alien-vampire couple in Fredric Brown's humorous vignette "Blood" (1955), who flee in a time machine to the unimaginably remote future in search of a safe haven. Like the "vampire as endangered species" in later fiction (notably Suzy McKee Charnas' *The Vampire Tapestry*, discussed in the next chapter), Einar illustrates the vulnerability of the untamed predator in the modern world. He also suffers the limitations of a nonhuman creature attempting to exist in the shadowed corners of human society. He has to change his diet in deference to his wife's sensibilities, keep his wings under control to avoid breaking things, and, above all, never fly where he might be seen by people other than his wife and children. Discontented despite his love for them, he finds himself reduced to helping Brunilla by flying wet laundry on a clothesline. The "captive thunder" (197) of his wings epitomizes his bitterness at feeling himself "nothing more than a summer sun-parasol, green and discarded" (196), an ironic characterization in view of his longing for his lost nocturnal freedom. He discovers a way of flying safely in the open sky when his children enter a kite contest. Holding the twine in his teeth, he poses as a kite, "a great and magical exclamation point across a cloud" (198). Despite the exultant tone of that final line, the predominant subtext of the story emphasizes limitation and sacrifice. Though love bestows compensations, still Einar's life consists of a compromise with his handicap. His plight suggests a member of an ethnic minority striving for fulfillment in camouflage and assimilation.

A late-twentieth-century tribute anthology, *The Bradbury Chronicles* (1991), updates Einar and Timothy in a pair of revisionist stories that allow them to triumph over their limitations. "The Obsession", by William Relling, Jr., thrusts the Family into the aggressively late-twentieth-century milieu of a television talk show. The program's producer, the allusively named Mr. Harker, is thrilled with "the discovery of an honest-to-goodness vampire living in Mellin Town,

Illinois" (94). His concept of Uncle Einar as "Dracula himself right here on our stage", conceived as "the perfect Halloween theme", trivializes the aliens among us by calculating projected ratings in comparison with "the skinhead transvestite born-again heroin addicts" (94). When Einar, his son Ronald, and Timothy (now an adult) appear on the show, the Host (not otherwise named) badgers them about their vampiric habits and, in stereotypical talk-show host fashion, overrides their attempts at coherent statements. Finally Einar manages to explain, "The Family comes in all shapes and sizes... We've been co-existing for centuries, living with you side-by-side without your being aware that we were any different from you" (101). In contrast to his assimilationist behavior in Bradbury's tale, here he shows pride in his racial heritage. His contention that humanity has "nothing at all to fear" (101) from the Family is borne out by the actions of the Host, who turns out to be arguably the most "evil" character in the story. The Host presents, as a surprise guest, one Barnard Voorhees, great-grandson of the man on whom Stoker's Van Helsing was based, just as Count Dracula was partly based on Einar. Instead of precipitating a violent on-camera confrontation with Einar, Voorhees, in the grip of his insane (not "evil") obsession, drives a stake into the heart of the Host. This character, guilty of feeding upon the misery of others, perishes like a traditional monster of folklore, while the "honest-to-goodness vampire" fills the role of victim--victimized by the distortions and trivialization of popular culture.

In the same anthology, Chelsea Quinn Yarbro's "Salome" introduces Timothy, as a young man, into the contemporary subgenre of vampire romance. In discovering his true love, he also discovers that he is more like the rest of the Family than they or he had supposed, a "late bloomer" rather than a defective (151). "'Until I met Leigh-Ann,' he muses, 'I didn't know I'd be able to do this [hypnotize a donor and drink her blood] at all. All the time I was growing up, I never wanted to, or needed to'" (152). Yarbro reinterprets the vampire's feeding from predation to eroticism. Timothy reassures the overprotective cat, Salome, of his harmlessness, and tells her, "This is one of the ways my family shows it when they like people" (152)--a matter-of-fact explanation diametrically opposite in tone from the revulsion with which Moore infuses the erotic encounter between Northwest Smith and Shambleau. Yarbro's story ends with a mutually passionate embrace between Timothy and Leigh-Ann, a conclusion unlikely--although not quite impossible, as William Tenn's "She Only Goes Out at Night" demonstrates--in mid-century pulp fiction.

"She Only Goes Out at Night" (1956) draws upon the stereotype of the seductive female vampire of popular culture, ultimately derived from Le Fanu's Carmilla and Stoker's Lucy, to undercut that stereotype by portraying its vampire heroine as a figure of pathos. Her blood craving is framed as a disease, which, as an inherited condition, controllable but not curable, sets her apart from normal humanity. Since "the vampire taint is inherited, usually just one child in a family getting it" (406), the vampire, though dangerous, is not responsible for his or her "taint". Neither quite human nor completely inhuman, this kind of vampire stands poised on the boundary between our kind and the Other. Tenn's narrative strategy in this story also frees his heroine from the "monster" role by relegating her predatory behavior to secondhand reportage; we never actually see her preying upon the children whose illness she causes. The narrator, Tom, works for a country doctor, whose son, Steve, falls in love with the sweet but mysterious Tatiana. Although, like Lucy, she victimizes children, Tatiana struggles with guilt over her blood-thirst and is careful not to take too much from any one victim. Tom, half Romanian, infers Tatiana's secret by recalling the lore he learned from his Transylvanian mother. He represents peasant wisdom, able to recognize the signs of vampirism. In contrast to Tom's folk beliefs about the evil of this phenomenon, Steve and the doctor view the condition from a scientific perspective, as "a sickness like any other sickness" (406).

Once vampirism is redefined as an illness instead of a diabolical curse, the doctor can treat it with "tinted glasses", "hormone injections", and a nightly dose made from dehydrated blood, no more remarkable than a diabetic's insulin (407). As demonstrated by her attempts to avoid harming her child victims, her initial refusal to marry Steve, and her attempted suicide, Tatiana is not demonic but capable of moral choice. Tenn reinterprets the Lucy Westenra figure, drinking the blood of children, as a victim of flawed genes rather than a creature of Hell. Where the protagonists of *Dracula* first perceive the mystery of Lucy's illness in medical terms and gradually shift to a supernatural interpretation, Tenn's narrator begins by assuming the supernatural, demonic nature of vampirism and concludes by embracing a medical explanation. Tom, the reader's surrogate, begins with the assumption, derived from folklore and reinforced by *Dracula,* that vampires are inherently evil. As he learns better, he leads the reader through the process of enlightenment along with him. He recognizes that Tatiana is "enough in love with [Steve] to try to kill herself the *only* way a vampire could be killed" (407, Tenn's emphasis). Expecting "one of these siren dames" (the seductive "vamp" of film conventions), Tom instead meets "a very frightened, very upset young lady" (407). Thus the vampire becomes humanized through Tatiana's ethical, self-sacrificing behavior and the emphasis on her youth and vulnerability. Unlike many vampire lovers in contemporary fiction, however, Tatiana must suppress the nonhuman facets of her nature to become worthy of "living happily ever after" (407). She becomes "Mrs. Steven Judd", who, every night, "shakes some powder into a tall glass of water, drops in an ice cube or two and has her daily blood toddy" (407)--domesticated from a legendary monster into just another suburban housewife.

Tenn's "The Human Angle" (1948) is one of several child vampire tales published at this period. Although her precise nature is not defined, the nameless little girl's status as a vampire daughter of vampire parents hints that she belongs to a nonhuman species. To journalist John Shellinger, in search of "a weepy individual slant on bloodsucking" in a "hill-billy" setting, all the people of the area seem alien (132). He sees them as stereotypes, inhabitants of a "pappy-mammy country where nobody speaks to strangers nohow" (132). When he picks up a rain-drenched little girl on a deserted road, he views her as potential copy, a source of the "human angle" he needs for his story, a simple farm child brave enough to venture out after dark despite the local vampire scare. He patronizingly explains vampire superstitions to her, intrigued by her unique definition of a vampire as "someone who needs people instead of meals" (134). While Shellinger spouts platitudes about silver bullets, stakes, and the belief that if "by nature, they [vampires] do such horrible things [killing children]...any way of getting rid of them is right," the girl simply insists, "No. You shouldn't drive stakes through people" (135). She holds to the credo of "live and let live", since "some people can't help what they are" (135). She proves more "human" in attitude than Shellinger, who dismisses vampires, if they exist, as monsters fit only for destruction, and views the hill people through the filter of his preconceptions. Ironically, his inability to see the child as she really is fuels his misapprehension that she fears the hypothetical monster; therefore he finds himself unprepared and defenseless when she bites into his throat. Although her attack upon Shellinger vitiates the pathos generated by her waiflike appearance and her reasoned arguments in favor of tolerance, the journalist's unappealing personality ensures that the weight of reader sympathy remains with the vampire child.

Richard Matheson uses a different strategy to generate empathy for his child narrator in "Dress of White Silk" (1951). A naive protagonist whose comprehension falls far short of the reader's, the little girl, because of her youth and inexperience, remains ignorant of the meaning of her own revelations. Her diction and the printed text's lack of apostrophes portray her as very young. The opening sentences of the story's second paragraph foreground both her tender age and her limited understanding: "Granma locked me in my room and wont let me out. Because its happened she says. I guess I was bad" (267). The orphaned narrator enjoys visiting her late mother's bedroom and playing with the mother's dress. One day she shows the dress and her mother's photograph to a friend, Mary Jane, who objects to the darkness in the house. Representing the viewpoint of the "normal" outside world, Mary Jane says that the mother's room "smells like sick people" (270), the dress "smells like garbage" and "has a hole in it," and the adored mother has "buck teeth" and "funny hands" (271). The dress then takes possession of the narrator, who remembers only a sense of being "like grown up strong" (271). In conclusion, locked in her bedroom, she defiantly claims that her grandmother "doesnt have to even give me supper. Im not hungry anyway. Im full" (272).

The reader, more sophisticated in vampire lore than the narrator, can fill the lacunae in the text. Supported by the other cues, the darkness in the house suggests, by analogy, the darkness of the tomb. We know the traditional association between vampires and the stench of decay, strongly emphasized in *Dracula,* and we recognize the hole in the white silk dress as the mark of a stake. We decode the mother's "buck teeth" and "funny hands" as fangs and claws. We infer that during the gap in the little girl's memory, she drank the blood of her playmate. Her incomprehension arouses sympathy; she acts from instinct, not malice. Her orphaned status, emphasized by her solitary play in the darkened house, also predisposes the reader to pity her. As for the grandmother, she transgresses conventional morality to shelter her daughter's child. She obviously knows about the lethal inheritance carried by the little girl but takes no preventive action, aside from the vain prohibition against entering the dead woman's bedroom. The grandmother "cries about the dress" and says of her deceased daughter, "I should burn it up but I loved her so" (269). In denial about her daughter's true nature, the grandmother constantly tells the child that her "momma is in heaven" (267). Like the narrator's limited understanding, the grandmother's willful blindness absolves her of intentional malice. Both characters, with their shared love for the dead woman, evoke more empathy than Mary Jane, with her callous taunting. As in "Homecoming", the "normal" point of view is marginalized while the "monstrous" dominates the center.

In "Drink My Red Blood" (1951), by contrast, Matheson uses an omniscient narrator to maintain an ironic distance from the boy protagonist, Jules. This story foreshadows the numerous demonic children in more recent works such as *Rosemary's Baby, The Exorcist,* and *The Omen,* which exploit adult uneasiness about the often incomprehensibly alien, as well as ruthlessly self-centered, behavior of partially socialized children. From the opposite viewpoint, "Drink My Red Blood" also dramatizes many growing children's sense of themselves as misfits within their own families. Like a changeling foisted on a human household by malevolent elves, Jules appears to be a vampire boy brought up by unsuspecting human parents. The narrative hesitates between psychological and paranormal explanations for Jules' aberrations, with the former dominant until the surprise reversal at the climax. (Just as with the similar ambiguity in "The Horla", I assume for the sake of argument that Jules' final epiphany represents objective truth within the text, not a delusion on his part; Matheson's omniscient narrative voice, I believe, supports this reading.) Neighborhood rumors reduce him to a freak or an urban legend rather than a normal child. People claim as "common knowledge that he was born on a night when winds uprooted trees", that "he was born with three teeth", which "he'd used to fasten himself on his mother's breast drawing blood with the milk" (162). Jules' parents, bewildered by his oddities, try to rationalize or suppress them, afraid he may be blind "until the doctor told them it was just a vacuous stare", considering him retarded until he finally begins to speak at age five, with the word "Death" (163). They combat his interest in death, blood, and vampirism by vainly trying to prevent him from reading *Dracula* over and over; they finally give up on him when they cannot force him to go back to school. His renunciation of school follows his reading aloud of a composition entitled "My Ambition by Jules Dracula", in which he expresses his desire to grow up to be a vampire (166). While Jules' parents and teacher and the principal confer "in sepulchral tones" (167), trying to pigeonhole him in a comprehensible category, other parents distance themselves and their families from his aberration. At first they cannot believe the other students' reports of Jules' classroom outburst, but upon reflection "they thought what horrible children they'd raised if the children could make up such things" (167). Jules is stigmatized as Other in order to protect the perceived innocence of the town's children.

Depressed, obsessed with a search for "something; he didn't know what" (167)--perhaps his own kind--Jules comes upon a vampire bat at the zoo: "He felt in his heart that it was really a man who had changed" (168). The omniscient narrator gives no positive indication as to whether this belief constitutes, as most readers would assume, a mere delusion on Jules' part. Night after night, Jules sneaks away from home to work at the wire on the bat's cage. Finally he frees it, takes it to a deserted shack in an alley, and feeds it his blood, with the "frenzied" invocation, "Count!...Drink my red blood! Drink me!" (179). As his blood drains away, Jules appears to awaken to the delusional nature of his obsession: "Mists crept away in his brain. One by one like drawn veils" (171). He realizes that he is "lying half-naked on garbage and letting a flying bat drink his blood" (171). This psychological rationalization of his lifelong abnormality, however, does not constitute the narrative's last word. "Through dying eyes" Jules sees a "tall dark man" with eyes "like rubies", who calls him "My son" (171). If this repudiation of a psychological rationale in favor of literal vampiric parentage represents "fact" within the world of the story, the vampire child incarnates fear of alien races, creatures who look like us but are not "our kind", infiltrating the families of the "superior" race through miscegenation. How did Jules' family give birth to this inhuman offspring? Was his mother raped by a vampire? Or is Jules the product of recessive genes, a hereditary "taint", like Tenn's Tatiana? Or is he, perhaps, a changeling, insinuated into a normal family like a cuckoo planted in another bird's nest? Matheson's text offers no answer.

In Matheson's *I Am Legend* (1954) the human, through a reversal of what constitutes "normal" and "abnormal", at last becomes transformed into the Other. The protagonist's wife's return from the grave to attack her husband, who must lay her to rest in the traditional manner, is a classic vampire fiction scenario. Matheson, however, uses references to *Dracula* to undercut the traditional view of vampirism and highlight, by contrast, his own rational rather than supernatural approach to the creatures of legend. This novel pioneered, and still represents the most elaborate development of, the "vampirism as infectious disease" hypothesis. A bacterial plague leaves the protagonist, Robert Neville, as the only living man on earth, everyone else having been either killed or transformed. Neville mounts a solitary crusade against the vampires. David J. Skal compares this novel to Finney's *The Body Snatchers* as "a subtextual commentary on the anxious underside of American life in the fifties" (*V Is for Vampire*, 123). Neville's behavior problematizes the distinction between himself and the vampires over whom he claims superiority. As Nina Auerbach puts it, this novel "blurred the demarcation between its vampires and its singularly nasty hero too ruthlessly to be widely popular in the '50s" (138). Just as the traditional undead monster drains its victims' lives as they sleep by night, Neville stalks vampires to murder them in their daytime sleep. For information, he alternately reads *Dracula* and medical texts on blood diseases. Stoker's novel proves an unreliable source of knowledge full of superstitions without foundation, such as the beliefs that vampires have no reflections and cannot cross running water. Yet although Neville considers *Dracula* "a hodgepodge of superstitions and soap-opera clichés", he acknowledges that it holds one central truth: "The strength of the vampire is that no one will believe in him" (13). Guided by trial and error, sifting fact from legend, Neville spends his days staking the undead and his nights barricaded in his house. Finally, however, he meets a young woman who has contracted the disease without either dying or becoming a mindless undead; she and her companions live in symbiosis with a mutated form of the bacteria.

Early in the story, while Neville still cowers in his home, a near-savage (although one with access to advanced technological resources) stripped down to the exigencies of survival, he delivers a drunken monologue on the vampire as "a minority element if there ever was one" (15). "Vampires are prejudiced against", he mockingly lectures to himself (15). Vampires are "hated because they are feared", yet are their "needs any more shocking than the needs of other animals and men?" (15). Neville elaborates the mock defense, contrasting the vampire's bloodlust with the predation of human beings upon their own kind. He plays devil's advocate with no genuine sympathy for his transformed neighbors, though; their nightly attempts to lure him out and drain his blood leave no room for detente. Neville finishes his monologue with an ironic allusion to the most extreme interracial taboo: "Sure...but would you let your sister marry one?" (16). When the young woman he befriends reluctantly engineers his capture, his attitude toward the transmuted survivors shifts. She calls him "the last of the old race", and he, yielding to the inevitable, accepts the role, finally seeing the mutated vampires as "people", not monsters (120). At the last, with his death approaching, Neville realizes, "I'm the abnormal one now" (121). To the new race, he is "some terrible scourge they had never seen...an invisible specter who had left for evidence of his existence the bloodless bodies of their loved ones" (122). Through Neville's deathbed enlightenment, the reader comes to share the viewpoint of the alien Other.

Brian Stableford updates the vampirism-as-disease model into the era of AIDS in *The Empire of Fear* (1988). In the world of this novel, vampires have long since consolidated their hegemony; they rule as an aristocratic caste over ordinary mortals. Ultimately vampirism is discovered to be an infectious agent that alters the human genetic code. The virus was originally brought to Earth on a meteorite that landed in the depths of Africa, so that the transformed elite are almost literally aliens. The infection has spread throughout the world, like AIDS, out of Africa by means of sexual intercourse. Only the semen of an infected male can effect transformation, and all male vampires are created through homosexual intercourse. After superstitions about vampirism are replaced with scientific facts, immortality becomes available to all except the minority who are immune to the virus. Freed by synthetic nourishment from the need to drink live blood, the transformed population embraces a new world order. Stableford's novel ends, like *I Am Legend,* with the image of a mortal man barred from the immortal destiny of the vampire majority. Unlike Neville, however, Stableford's Michael is not a feared and loathed outcast, but the cherished lover of a vampire woman, so that this novel concludes with reconciliation rather than alienation.

The late-twentieth-century apocalyptic novel *AfterAge* (1993), by Yvonne Navarro, also pays homage to Matheson. In the world of Navarro's novel, just as in *I Am Legend,* vampirism has spread out of control, causing depopulation and the breakdown of society. In keeping with contemporary ecological awareness, Navarro portrays vampires who have outmultiplied their food supply, precipitating a disastrous crash in the numbers of the prey species. Instead of a solitary surviving resistor, the protagonists comprise a group of people who form an alliance to combat the vampires in an abandoned Chicago. The vampires, rather than constituting a monolithic force of destruction, quarrel among themselves, pursuing personal agendas, and one at least is humanized by her willingness to help the non-vampire survivors. The situation is further complicated by a third element, human traitors who collaborate with the vampires. Navarro's novel, unlike Matheson's and Stableford's, concludes with the total destruction of the undead, by means of a genetically engineered bacterium. In this world the renewal of society is symbolized by the birth of a completely human baby.

A different scenario for the potential evolution of a new species appears in Cyril M. Kornbluth's "The Mindworm" (1950). The plague in *I Am Legend* is tentatively attributed to the aftereffects of nuclear bomb tests, generating abnormal dust storms and perhaps causing mutations of insects (which spread the disease) and bacteria. Postwar nuclear anxiety is also reflected in the genetic abnormalities that spawn Kornbluth's Mindworm, conceived during a liaison between two naval officers on a ship near a tropical island during a bomb test. Both Matheson and Kornbluth attribute the evolution of a new--and predatory--species to human meddling with nature. The Mindworm, however, appears to be a unique specimen, cut off in his prime before he can breed more like himself. The omniscient narrator first frames the boy as another misfit child who awakens adult anxieties. His caretakers at the orphanage see him as "stupid, puny, and stubborn, greedy and miserable," in short, "an exceptionally unattractive-looking kid" (410). When he shows evidence of mind-reading talent, the orphanage director loses no time in placing him in a less than desirable adoptive home, where he stays only three months. After he runs away, the Mindworm--given no personal name, except the alias he later offers to one of his victims--becomes a full-fledged demon child who feeds on violent emotions, thereby killing the homeless men who try to assault him.

As an adult, he prowls from place to place in search of the "epicurean" pleasure of people he can find at or goad into "a ripe emotional crisis" (415). He lives upon psychic energy, supplemented only by water, and supplies himself with money by robbing the bodies of his victims. In contrast to the volatile passions of his victims, the Mindworm himself displays no emotion other than delight in feeding; he appears sociopathically detached from humanity. Whether this coldness arises from the rejection he experienced in childhood or from his essentially inhuman nature is left unclear. His identification by a generic rather than personal name emphasizes his uniqueness as well as his nonhuman traits. Confident of his superiority to those around him, he fears only the rare person with psychic gifts or extreme intelligence. His arrogance renders him blind to the danger of a "West Virginia coal and iron town" inhabited mostly by immigrants from Eastern Europe (416). He clings to the mistaken impression that these subliterate people are "stupid and safe" (417), an illusion promoted by the fact that he can understand only thoughts couched in languages known to him, so that the immigrants' thoughts are often incomprehensible. As befits his own technologically-based origin, he fears only sophisticated, educated people, who never suspect the existence of creatures like him. The people of the town, like Tom in "She Only Goes Out at Night", possess a different kind of knowledge, to which the Mindworm is vulnerable. Recognizing him as "wampyir", the "mustached old men" stake and behead him before he has time to realize "that what clever people have not yet learned, some quite ordinary people have not yet entirely forgotten" (419). Ironically contrasting scientific sophistication with the collective memory of the folk, Kornbluth uses the Mindworm's abbreviated life as a nuclear-age cautionary tale about the hazards of uncontrolled knowledge divorced from wisdom.

The vampire in "Share Alike" (1953) by Jerome Bixby and Joe E. Dean also represents a reinterpretation of the traditional monster in science-fiction-based terms, in this case morally neutral rather than, like the Mindworm, sociopathically destructive. After a shipwreck, Craig, the human protagonist, finds himself alone in a lifeboat with Eric Hofmanstahal, the vampire. Hofmanstahal, a Romanian with a "colorful past" (423), never eats his share of the rations. From these two details, along with Craig's increasing weakness, the reader infers the truth about the vampire before the protagonist does. Craig realizes what Hofmanstahal is when he awakens one night to find the other man at his throat. This vampire, however, is a member of the natural order, a representative of another species rather than a creature transformed by the Devil. By implication he contrasts himself with the sharks circling the boat, which "rend and kill, and give nothing in return for the food they so brutally take. They can offer only their bodies, which are in turn devoured by larger creatures" (424). The vampire, also a part of the food chain, at least refrains from killing Craig and rewards the younger man by ceding him the surplus food rations. Craig at first rejects this "symbiotic relationship" (426), as Hofmanstahal classifies it, but finally yields despite his qualms. Under the influence of his late father, a Baptist minister--who, though not physically present, functions in this tale as the Van Helsing figure who urges the exorcism of evil--Craig first interprets the vampire as a spawn of the Devil.

Like Tenn's narrator in "She Only Goes Out at Night", Craig, once he realizes that the "monster" is not supernatural and therefore not inherently evil, learns to see the vampire as an individual rather than a demon. The vampire disillusions Craig, literally, by deconstructing his illusions about vampirism. When, under the influence of popular culture, Craig challenges Hofmanstahal to turn himself into a bat, the vampire disclaims any such power. "Nor do I sleep in a coffin. Nor does daylight kill me," he says, dismissing the literary and cinematic conventions that distort human perceptions of his kind (426). He offers a range of natural explanations for his species' existence--perhaps they originated on another planet; perhaps (reminiscent of *Darker Than You Think*) "when *Homo sapiens* and the ape branched from a common ancestor, there was a third strain which was so despised by both that it was driven into obscurity"; perhaps vampires are "a species which was quite different from man but which, because of man's dominance over the earth, imitated him until it developed a physical likeness to him" (427). He scorns the theological hypothesis of the vampire's diabolical origin as a pernicious legend due to which his people "have been persecuted, imprisoned, burned alive...all because our body chemistry is unlike that of man" (427).

Making the familiar strange, forcing us to view ourselves through alien eyes, he points out that vampires "drink from the fountain of life while man feasts at the fleshpots of the dead, yet [vampires] are called monsters" (427). He compares humanity to the sharks that swarm around the boat. Thus he presents himself as a victim of persecution, revealing that his grandfather "died with a white ash stake through his heart" and maintaining, "We variants have more to fear from the ignorant and superstitious than they from us. There are so many of them, and so few of us" (426). Vampires are framed, therefore, as a persecuted minority race. In view of the intimacy between Craig and Hofmanstahal, the "almost lascivious" feeling of "comfortable warmth and lassitude" (427) that the vampire's bite confers upon Craig, and Hofmanstahal's "almost sexual avidity" (429) in feeding, homoerotic overtones cannot be ignored. Vampires are persecuted as "maniacs and perverts" (427), as well as a threatening alien species. Craig's initial reaction of nauseated revulsion, far out of proportion to Hofmanstahal's behavior, invites a reading of homophobia. This aspect of the relationship becomes clear when a ship finally appears on the horizon, and Hofmanstahal drinks "for the last time" to mark the end of the "little idyll" (429). Craig sees the approaching ship as a symbol of "[n]ormalcy and sanity, cities and machines and half-forgotten values" (429). The imagined phantom of his late father, the minister, arises to damn him for "lying in the arms of" a monster (430). In panic he struggles, throwing the vampire overboard to be killed instantly by the sharks. Although Craig immediately repents of killing his friend, the momentary lapse into a theological rather than naturalistic reading of vampirism transforms him into one of the persecutors. With his shift back to affection for the vampire, and the final exorcism of, not the "demon", but his father's image, Craig awakens to a "new awareness...coming over him in a hot flood" (430); repeated doses of Hofmanstahal's venom have transformed him into a vampire. Although the text does not explain the biological mechanism of this transmutation (given the vampire's status as a member of a separate species), Craig has become the Other he originally feared.

"Share Alike", as an early fictional instance of communication and mutuality between human and vampire, foreshadows the wide variety of "good" vampires found in the science fiction and fantasy of the late twentieth century. The next chapter will examine a selection of the most significant of these.

Chapter 3

Conversations with the Vampire
(Post-1970)

T he vampire, traditionally devoid of a reflection, often serves, paradoxically, as a mirror; the fictional monster reflects a distorted image of the feared and marginalized Other in the primary world. Our perception of the vampire, like our perception of "lower" animals and "different" fellow-humans, suffers the warping effects of projected guilt, hostility, and desire. The universe of Philip Jose Farmer's *Image of the Beast* (1968; 1969) is haunted by creatures that have entered our space-time continuum through "temporary breaks in the walls, accidental cracks" between our realm and other universes (131). Among these are the supernatural beings of earthly mythology, including vampires. "But they have forms so alien," one character explains, "that the human brain has no forms to fit them. And so the human brain gives them forms to *explain* them" (131, Farmer's emphasis).

Human beings do not merely perceive these alien invaders as vampires, werewolves, and so forth; rather, "It is a matter of the aliens actually being molded into these forms" (131). Whereas creatures such as the Horla and Williamson's witch-folk generate human cultures' superstitions, Farmer's monsters are shaped *by* human myth and legend. Alien vampires in contemporary fiction often acknowledge their dependence, however unwilling, upon humankind, and find themselves molded by human expectations and the stereotypical images that filter our perceptions of the inhuman. They suffer the postmodern quandary of beings whose essential nature depends upon others' belief. This chapter focuses on alien vampires who are deeply involved, whether willingly or not, with the human race.

The objective consequences of subjective beliefs and conflicting perspectives on the nature of reality shape human-vampire interaction in "A Cold Stake", by Phyllis Ann Karr (1991), which depicts a twofold cultural conflict. Set in the twenty-first century, this narrative contrasts preternatural creatures with ordinary human beings and "reality perceivers", who see the world in terms of "the legal definition of Standard Reality", with "fantasy perceivers" (138). Reality perceivers cannot recognize vampires for what they are. Observers need "a percentage of fantasy perception to see [the vampire's] fangs; to see that he was drinking blood when other people were drinking eggnog; to see his lack of a reflection" (144). The majority perceive the vampire as casting a reflection "and never understood that their eyes weren't registering it" (144). So-called reality perceivers, ironically, are blind to whatever facets of their environment do not fit into the consensus reality bound by the "legal definition". They view "fanciers" as "the immoral dirt of society", not simply people who "see things differently", but the instigators of social and natural disasters such as the great earthquake of 2029 (145).

Clement, the young vampire protagonist of the tale, clashes with Gary Wilson, a would-be "realizer" who wholeheartedly embraces the scapegoating of fanciers as well as the not-quite-human element of the population. Gary vacillates between disbelief in vampires and the impulse to stigmatize them as diabolical. Urged to make up his mind whether Clement is "a fancier or just a real vampire", Gary, in language suggestive of contemporary religious right-wing politics, rants, "He's a fancier vampire! And that makes him twice as evil and wicked and satanic" (144). Gary actually overreacts against the fantasy-perceiving world-view because of his own desperate longing to become certified (through the standard government test) as one of the reality-perceiving majority. His recognition of Clement's vampirism threatens Gary's self-image. To exorcise his own self-doubt, he tries to murder Clement with a breadstick, which he imagines to be a wooden stake, thus demonstrating his own unwanted "fancier" tendencies. After he does pass the official test with a high reality-perception score, Gary allows Clement to talk him into a truce. He promises never again "to attack anyone just because he or she is a vampire" and acknowledges that "wicked vampires" are morally no different from "wicked human beings" (156). This narrative exploration of the nature of reality and the value of imagination dramatizes the paradox that "the right kind of fantasy perception," required to see a vampire's true nature, is actually "the right kind of reality perception" (145). "One-hundred-and-one-percent reality perception--a secret, hidden percentage point beyond the grasp of Standard Reality" (145) reveals that the mundane universe known to the majority constitutes only a small portion of "reality". Under Clement's influence, Gary comes to accept the world-view of "fanciers" and nonhuman citizens as valid.

Dissonance between the dominant cultural consensus and objective reality also pervades an older story, "Vanishing Breed" (1970), by Niel Straum. The thesis that the Earth-dwelling humanoids known as vampires have an extraterrestrial origin (as opposed to the motif of vampires openly invading from other planets) has appeared in several novels and stories of the late twentieth century. "Vanishing Breed" is, however, the earliest of which I am aware. The creatures in this tale, set in an unspecified future century, suffer a blurring of their identity, a confusion between themselves and *Homo sapiens*. The youngest generation, vampire-human hybrids known as "vamps", have internalized human beliefs about their kind. They accept the erroneous premise that vampires are the undead, human beings transformed. Only the eldest of their race remember the full history of their origin on a distant planet. Their story has been told, instead, by the dominant human species, in distorted form through superstition, legend, sensational fiction, and horror films. The protagonist, Carl, one of the vamps, has been assimilated so thoroughly into human society that he cannot bring himself to leave when all the others flee from our solar system.

In Colin Wilson's *The Space Vampires* (1976), the psychic-vampire extraterrestrial invaders find their counterparts already dwelling on Earth as one thread in the web of terrestrial biology. This novel was preceded by a pair of earlier works, *The Mind Parasites* (1967) and *The Philosopher's Stone* (1969), which explore similar themes. *The Mind Parasites* begins, like *Sinister Barrier*, with the mysterious death of a scientist who has discovered the existence of psychic vampires preying upon humankind. Wilson's "parasites" have not warped the entire course of terrestrial history, like Russell's Vitons and Williamson's witch-folk, but have corrupted and weakened the human creative spirit since the late eighteenth century. For the past two centuries, the mind vampires have been "destroying the human power of self-renewal" (61) by draining energy and even, in some cases, taking over a human mind to use it for their purposes. Wilson's narrator, in discovering and combating the parasites who lurk in humanity's collective unconscious, expands his mental and psychic abilities to a nearly supernatural degree. Because he has realized the full potential of his mind, in him the "cancer" of the mind vampires is "slowly dying of starvation" (170). *The Philosopher's Stone* also develops the theme of the discovery and expansion of previously hidden mental powers, with suggestions that the influence of Lovecraftian "elder races" has blocked humanity from reaching its full potential. The specifically predatory dimension of these motifs reaches its fullest expression in *The Space Vampires.*

In this novel biologists of a near-future era have learned how to measure the "life field" of organisms with "lambda meters" (54). The feeding of predators involves the absorption of the prey's life force; however, sexual intercourse also entails a measurable transfer of energy. Predatory behavior, "negative vampirism", aims at "total destruction of the victim. But in the case of sex, there is also positive vampirism" (59). Normal sexual relations are characterized by a psychic tension in which, ideally, "one life field can actually reinforce another" (59). Carlsen, head of the expedition that discovers the alien ship (which is significantly referred to as the Stranger), enjoys direct experience of energy exchange through sexual intercourse but later finds that his contact with the aliens has stimulated his latent vampiric qualities. As he perceives the situation, the alien predator has converted him into a vampire and awakened in him "abnormal desires" along with "the power to carry them out" (127). Count Geijerstam, one of the novel's Van Helsing-like authorities on vampirism, insists that Carlsen has simply "become aware of the vampirism that exists in all human beings" and praises Carlsen for his ability to replenish his partner's energy as well as consume it (127). As Veronica Hollinger points out, Geijerstam is analogous to Dracula as well as Van Helsing, for Wilson's Count lives in a castle with three beautiful young women who practice "positive vampirism" under his guidance.

Despite this potentially affirmative view of vampirism as symbiotic exchange, the predatory model, with thoroughly negative implications, dominates the text. Although vampirism has existed on Earth all along, an inescapable pattern in terrestrial ecology, kinship between human and alien is deemphasized; the invaders are framed as the threatening Other, to be expelled or exterminated. Harking back to Finney's *Body Snatchers,* Wilson's aliens stalk unseen among us by possessing the bodies of human hosts. Carlsen experiences the alien's attempt to "enter his nervous system and sever it from his will", to make him "a prisoner in his own brain, unable to move" (174). Through this life-or-death struggle Carlsen realizes, "They were enemies; nothing could change that" (174). Earlier speculations that the aliens have been "the secret mentors of humankind" (83) come to nothing. As Hollinger observes, the text associates vampirism with negative imagery such as "sexual perversion" (49), "a Venus flytrap closing on an insect" (146), "galactic criminals" and "lepers" (194), "a despot with limitless powers" (197), and the witches in "Hansel and Gretel" and *The Wizard of Oz* (199). The sexual dimension of vampirism is presented in sadomasochistic terms, for example, when Carlsen vampirizes a woman who has been possessed by an alien: "He did as she asked, brutally draining her energy as if intent on destroying her"--a process that brings the willing victim to orgasm (166). Although the space vampires occupy both male and female bodies throughout the story, vampiric phenomena are most often associated with the feminine; Hollinger notes that "Wilson's text seems to perceive the sexually active woman as somehow linked to the alien forces which threaten from 'out there'" (13). *The Space Vampires* resembles *Dracula* in its "binary thinking", which is, in Hollinger's words, "rigidly hierarchical" and in which "one of the terms is privileged over the other, Inside over Outside, Human over Alien, Masculine over Feminine" (14).

Jacqueline Lichtenberg's vampires in *Those of My Blood* (1988), the "luren", also have an interstellar origin despite their long residence on Earth. Lichtenberg's critical and authorial stance, as noted in the introduction, privileges connection and mutual exchange over detachment and hostility. Her vampires must learn to deal with humanity as a sentient species deserving respect; "understanding", as Lichtenberg remarks in "Vampire with Muddy Boots", is "the key to the solution of the problem" (4). During their centuries on our world, the luren in *Those of My Blood* have divided into two groups, Residents and Tourists. Though not completely assimilated into the human population, Residents recognize the ethical claims of humanity and try to refrain from exploiting their non-luren neighbors. They nourish themselves with cloned blood rather than preying on the living. Tourists, on the other hand, regard human beings as livestock or prey. Their contempt for humanity, however, ironically entails self-contempt, since all present-day terrestrial vampires of both factions are hybrids, the product of interspecies breeding. The imminent arrival of a luren spaceship brings the conflict between the two groups to a crisis. The protagonist, Titus, a Resident, wants to thwart the Tourists' project of contacting the luren ship and revealing the vampires' presence on Earth, an act that the Residents fear will lead to the subjection of humanity. The antagonist, Abbot, cannot be called a villain, for he does only what he thinks necessary for the survival of his people, with no unnecessary harm to others. "If humans discover us before rescue arrives," he berates Titus, "they'll slaughter us--just as they did in Transylvania" (29). Though he has none of Titus' scruples about manipulating and preying on human beings, he never behaves cruelly. Their rivalry is complicated by the fact that Abbot is Titus' "father" in the vampire life, who nourished Titus with his own blood after Titus' first death. When the alien ship arrives, bearing a single luren survivor, H'lim, Titus and Abbot find themselves trapped in an uneasy alliance to deal with the interstellar visitor who, though warily friendly, views them as weakened by their hybrid heritage, not true luren. H'lim regards human beings, because of their unique psychic qualities, as a "genetic gold mine" (313). As for the human scientists, unaware of Titus and Abbot's kinship with the extraterrestrial, they cautiously acknowledge, "*This* blood-sucking monster from outer space turned out to be a nice guy" (316, Lichtenberg's emphasis). Each side in the multivalent conflict pursues its own agenda for legitimate, though self-interested, motives.

Lichtenberg's aliens use a form of telepathy known as Influence, through which the vampire can manufacture illusions and make an unwary human victim accept any distortion of reality as fact. Partly because of Influence and partly through the innate magnetism Lichtenberg's vampires project when hungry, they are sexually irresistible. Titus discovers that his human lover, Inea, has the power to infuse his reconstituted blood drink with her "ectoplasm" (life force), giving him satisfaction unattainable from the lifeless fluid in itself. Before they copulate, Inea asks him, "Is it especially good with--vampires? Or is that a myth, too?"; he tells her, "I'll make it like nothing you've ever known" (95). He keeps that promise, using his power to coax her body's energy to its highest pitch before seeking his own pleasure, acting out--like many contemporary fictional vampires--the feminine fantasy of the perfectly attentive lover whose fulfillment depends on his partner's. At the moment of Inea's climax, Titus feels "the intense surge of ectoplasm, as if energy had come into her from nowhere and she had made it living substance for him to feed on" (119). He tells her in the midst of their lovemaking, "If you let me do this for you properly, all I took when you let me drink will be restored and more" (118). His avowal, "I live in your love and wither without it" (119), makes clear the mutuality of his kind of vampirism, similar to Wilson's "positive vampirism" but without the ambivalence found in the earlier novel. The erotic hyperpotency of vampires carries no negative connotations in Lichtenberg's narrative, unlike *The Space Vampires* and earlier works such as "Shambleau".

In contemporary fiction vampire sexuality more often signifies intimacy rather than exploitation. As Judith E. Johnson observes, particularly for women writers of vampire fiction "the sexual relationship implied by the vampire's kiss is more an exchange of passion than a rape," and blood represents not "a source of horror but...a source of power, a source of the ability to share love and create life" (78). In *Those of My Blood* Titus' symbiotic copulation with Inea illustrates the possibility of non-destructive, even beneficial energy exchange. The supreme satisfaction, Titus discovers, requires "total commitment, both from the luren and from the human", rather than exploitation of prey by predator (156). And even the triangular tension among Titus, Abbot, and H'lim functions in terms of compromise and reciprocity rather than open hostility. Lichtenberg's treatment of vampiric strengths illustrates Joan Gordon's thesis that female authors tend to employ a model of power that "does not involve a rigid chain of command", or, for that matter, threats of force, but instead "focuses on cooperation and endurance" (230). In this model, vampires, while still "associated with power, no longer hold threatening positions...they become super-survivors instead of super-killers" (230)--a thesis we shall see demonstrated with particular complexity by Suzy McKee Charnas' *The Vampire Tapestry*. The violent conclusion of *Those of My Blood* results from a series of unfortunate accidents rather than from malice aforethought. After the deaths of Abbot and H'lim temporarily postpone the problem of whether to deal with the luren home world, Titus summarizes the novel's message: "Nonhuman people are out there... Now more than ever we have to *learn* about the galaxy... Maybe there can be peaceful contact eventually" (400). Alien races have become "people" rather than monsters.

A similar subtext pervades Lichtenberg's Sime-Gen series, beginning with *House of Zeor* (1974). In the distant future, humankind has mutated into two subspecies, Gens, who produce an objectively measurable life energy called "selyn", and Simes, who must draw this substance from Gens once a month or die of "need". While the tentacles on the Simes' forearms visibly mark them as alien, Gens, as producers of selyn, are in fact equally different from the Ancients (present-day *Homo sapiens*). As Lichtenberg explains in "The 'Kill'/'Need' Convention", an article for the periodical *Ambrov Zeor*, "Though Simes and Gens are both human, their biological imperatives are different enough that to Ancients they are essentially nonhuman" (6-7). Her aim in writing the series, she states in the same article, has been "to open that window into another reality where the laws of the universe proclaim a lack of compassion to be a capital offense, a sentence that is carried out instantaneously and without due process" (7). The Simes' energy draining carries vampiric overtones, of course, and in the opening scene of *House of Zeor,* the Gen protagonist, Hugh Valleroy, sees the Sime, Klyd, as "a gaunt-winged vampire" in a cape (13). Hugh, born of a mother who escaped from Sime Territory to live among free Gens, quickly reminds himself, "Simes were only human mutants who wore riding capes for comfort" (13). The tension between "monster" and "only human" dominates the series. Most Gens fear Simes because the drawing of selyn ordinarily kills the victim; as a rule, only "channels" such as Klyd can take selyn harmlessly and transfer it to non-channels. The average Gen, therefore, regards Simes as terrifying demons. Simes, conversely, must view Gens as no more than talking animals, since a Sime's survival depends on being able to kill a Gen every month. Each side dehumanizes the other.

Since Gens externally resemble Ancients (us), the Gen protagonist, Hugh, forced into reluctant cooperation with Klyd on an undercover mission into

Sime Territory, serves as the reader's surrogate. Through Hugh's experiences, we move from the initial view of Simes as vampiric monsters to recognition of their humanity. Gradually he becomes aware, through his growing friendship with Klyd, of the possibility of mutually beneficial interdependence between Sime and Gen. The novel and the series as whole develop the thesis that Sime and Gen are meant to be complementary. The Gen supplies selyn and gains, in return, enhanced physical health, while the Sime, in exchange for the vital energy that the Gen can easily spare, gives the protection of his or her superhuman strength and preternatural sensory perception. On the surface Simes appear the more powerful by far, yet "in any transfer situation [exchange of selyn], the Gen always has the upper hand" (158). This reciprocity is symbolized, in the era of *House of Zeor,* by the Householdings, kibbutzlike associations of Simes and Gens living and working together under the leadership of a channel. On a personal level, "victim" becomes reinterpreted as "donor", and at the novel's climax, when Hugh donates selyn to Klyd, he sees in the Sime "not a ferocious predator intent on murder, but his partner" (219). Moreover, Hugh feels a sense of oneness with Klyd and experiences a "demand that seemed at once to be so bottomless and so much his own" followed by "a double satisfaction that soothed both halves of him"; he knows himself as "both giver and receiver in that interchange" (219). Through their shared "Intimate Adventure" (in Lichtenberg's phrase), Sime and Gen cease to dehumanize each other and progress from hostility to mutuality.

Dan Simmons uses the genetic mutation model to explore the potential emergence of a new species in *Children of the Night* (1992). The novel begins in Romania during the chaos following the downfall of the Ceausescu regime. An American doctor, Kate Neuman, adopts Joshua, an orphaned infant suffering from a bizarre blood disease. At home in the United States, she discovers the unique powers of regeneration that accompany his damaged immune system.

The phenomenal healing capacity of Joshua's blood, however, depends upon constant nourishment by the blood of others. Although Kate supplies this need through transfusion, customarily the sufferers from this syndrome drain blood directly from human victims. Agents of the extended family to which Joshua belongs kidnap him and return him to Romania. Kate undertakes a quest to rescue him, not only for his own sake, but also for his blood, which holds the promise of a cure for AIDS and many other lethal maladies. A "cellular or physiological mutation in that family" gives their bodies the power to "cannibalize genetic material from donor blood so that their own immunodeficiency was overcome" (115). A "blood-rich shadow organ" in the alimentary canal enables Joshua's kin to utilize "human blood as a regular mechanism" (115). "A small royal family...requiring secrecy due to the nature of their disease and their crimes, having the money and power necessary to eliminate enemies and retain their secrecy" can and do perpetuate their bloodline through the centuries (168).

Because the principal representative of the vampire clan in this novel is a seven-month-old baby, the condition does not brand its carriers as "evil". Set against the horrors of the Ceausescu era, graphically depicted in the filthy, overcrowded orphanages of Romania, the need to consume human blood appears less terrible. "The banality of evil" in human history is illustrated by the premise that "Dracula would be a story. The plight of hundreds of thousands of victims of political madness, bureaucracy, stupidity" is merely an "inconvenience" (28). Even Vlad Tepes, patriarch of the "Family of Night" (35), the late dictator's "Dark Advisor" (27), does not seem utterly villainous, since the narrative presents him mainly as a sick, tired old man. Despite Joshua's destiny as the "next Prince of the *Voivoda Strigoi*" (212), because he is also an innocent child, he invites sympathy rather than horror from the reader.

Kate offers Vlad an escape from his clan's centuries-old existence of secrecy and predation, for she can cure the "family disease...while offering you a substitute for the human blood you have had to steal" and "a chance to help humanity rather than prey on it" (318). Moreover, the hemoglobin substitute she has synthesized mitigates the "hormonal and mood-altering effects" that have made the carriers of the mutation behave like monsters (318). Kate's escape with baby Joshua, the "Prince" of the "Family of Night", symbolizes the hope that an ancient evil may be converted to beneficial purposes. At the conclusion, Vlad muses, "I have been a source of terror to my people and employees many times in my long life. I know now that I would have welcomed being a savior to my people. Perhaps, through this child" (378-79).

Susan Petrey's Varkela, a blood-drinking tribe of the Russian steppes, offer a rare example of a completely benign vampiric race. They appear to be a subspecies of *Homo sapiens,* since they frequently interbreed with human females (their own women often dying at puberty from a sex-linked recessive condition). They earn their modest monthly ration of human blood by selling their skills as horse-tamers and shamanistic healers. Like Lichtenberg's channels, Petrey's characters acquire their necessary sustenance through mutually beneficial exchange, not theft or rape. The Varkela physician Vaylance, in search of training in Western-style medicine in "The Healer's Touch", reminds himself that "one could not ask for blood unless one had earned through healing" and reflects with shame on the prospect that he may "have to stoop to blood-theft in the night to feed his need" (53). The open-minded Russian doctor Rimsky discovers Vaylance's secret and fearlessly offers blood in payment for the Varkela's shamanistic treatment of a mentally disturbed girl. As a scientist, Rimsky perceives that Vaylance represents "a subspecies of *Homo sapiens*", rather than a creature of the Devil, and delights in the possibility that he has "stumbled on a new race--must write this up and send it to a scientific journal" (53). On the other hand, he recognizes the danger posed by superstition and vows to conceal Vaylance's true nature from people with "more imagination than brains" who would equate him with "the mythical Vampire" (59).

Like the luren and many other fictional vampires, the Varkela have extraordinary sexual prowess. They possess the ability to "bewitch" women with the hypnotic song they use to calm patients during healing. In "Leechcraft" Vaylance has no need to draw upon this power when he lies with Myrna, a woman he meets in a "dreamwalk" across time to modern America. Somewhat like Elaine Bergstrom's vampires (discussed below), he shares visions with her and tries to teach her to dreamwalk. The vampiric telepathy or empathy imagined by Lichtenberg, Bergstrom, and Petrey bridges the gulfs between sexes, races, and species in a mode and with a completeness impossible (so far as we know) in real life. Myrna finds Vaylance to be "the most sensitive lover she had ever known" (126). Sharing his blood with her, he tells her, "Our souls have touched" (127) and sees in her "the wolvish soul" that "may be befriended, never tamed" (128). Again we notice how the hyperpotent sexuality of the Other, a source of horror and revulsion in *Dracula*, "Shambleau", and *Darker Than You Think*, is transformed by contemporary fiction into a positive quality. Carol A. Senf maintains that "the change in the vampire motif" toward a more sympathetic rendering is "directly linked to changing attitudes toward sexuality" (162). Characters in contemporary vampire fiction, both human and nonhuman, "recognize their full potential as individuals" as including "the right to choose a fulfilling sexual relationship", and they "openly acknowledge that sexuality is a healthy and normal response, not a threat to the individual or the society" (162-163).

If human characters in these stories are fascinated with the vampire's erotic magnetism and alluring otherness, vampires, from a variety of motives, are also irresistibly drawn to human beings. Joshua's race in George R. R. Martin's *Fevre Dream* (1982) has no culture of its own, aside from a myth of a vampire kingdom that perished in a remote prehistoric age; they borrow everything from humanity, even language. Yet their bond with the human species consists of more than cultural parasitism and thirst for blood. Joshua reflects, "We killed you easily, and took joy in it, for we found beauty in you, and always my people had been drawn to beauty. Perhaps it was your likeness to us we found so captivating" (159). This fascination exists apart from need for blood, since only after inventing an artificial blood-substitute (freeing himself and his followers from the compulsion to kill once a month) does Joshua seek alliance and ultimately friendship with the riverboat captain Abner Marsh. Elaine Bergstrom's vampires, the Austra clan, gravitate toward human lovers and, most of the time, feel little sexual attraction toward their own kind. When an Austra male and a human female mutually exchange blood--an intimacy that is taboo yet strangely alluring for the vampires--fertile mating can occur. Offspring or descendants of these rare unions, like Lichtenberg's human-luren hybrids, can become true vampires, given the right conditions. In Petrey's series, male Varkela, as noted above, often mate with ordinary women. In "The Healer's Touch", we learn that for a male Varkela "to impregnate a human female was regarded as a sign of especial virility" (39). Clearly, the sexual fascination of the Other works in both directions.

Some alien vampires manage to remain true to their essential natures while coexisting with, even loving, human associates. Joshua in Martin's *Fevre Dream* has an anomalous childhood that predisposes him to regard human beings as more than prey. Orphaned by his father's execution during the French Reign of Terror, he knows little of his true nature; he has been taught the superiority of his family over ordinary people, and he knows he must avoid daylight, but the "red thirst"--the monthly need for blood--comes upon him only at the age of twenty, adolescence for his kind. Having always considered himself "superior", he now decides that instead he is "something unnatural, a beast, a soulless monster" (149). He explains to his human ally, Captain Abner Marsh, "In English, your kind might call me vampire, werewolf, witch, warlock, sorcerer, demon, ghoul...I do not like those names. I am none of them... We have no name for ourselves" (143). His race depends for their identity upon the distortions promulgated by those they call "cattle" (144). Imbued with human morality, Joshua feels guilt for his acts and, in despair, futilely attempts suicide. "To atone," he finally resolves, "I must live, bring life and beauty and hope back into the world to take the place of all that I had taken" (153). Having become "endlessly weary of the mistrust between our races" (144), he acknowledges an ethical obligation to humanity despite the differences between the two species. He devotes his life to learning not to kill (by inventing a potion to substitute for living blood), destroys a vampire rival who wants to maintain the old, savage ways, and makes a true friend of Abner Marsh. The importance of this relationship to Joshua is demonstrated by his eventually placing an elaborate tombstone on Marsh's grave and visiting the site regularly for decades thereafter.

In contrast to the difference between human and vampire, culturally imposed differences among human beings appear trivial. Joshua comments on the exclusion and destruction of human beings by their own kind in the name of superstition and prejudice: "I have seen your race burn old women because they were suspected of being one of us, and here in New Orleans I have witnessed the way you enslave your own kind, whip them and sell them like animals simply because of the darkness of their skin. The black people are closer to you, more kin, than ever my kind can be. You can even get children on their women, while no such interbreeding is possible between night and day" (162). Again, the image of a vampire race living among us places human differences in perspective. Because human society persecutes its own kind on the basis of superficial distinctions, Joshua knows it would not be safe for his race to come out of hiding; breaching their secrecy would invite extermination. The horrors of war and the crimes of such infamous individuals as Vlad Tepes and the woman who "whipped her maids and bled them...and rubbed the blood into her skin to preserve her beauty" (163)--a clear reference to Elisabeth Bathory--stand in contrast to the vampires' periodic killing for the blood necessary to their survival. Human criminals such as Countess Bathory commit murder because of "an evil nature", a far worse sin than acting under "compulsion" (163). On the other hand, Joshua's detached view of humanity enables him to recognize the "enlightened" members of the human race, "men of science and learning" with the potential for acceptance and cooperation between the two species (162).

The eponymous narrator of Tanith Lee's *Sabella* (1980) comes to terms with human-alien interaction in a different way. Similar to Joshua, she grows up thinking herself human but aberrant. As a Terran child living on an Earth-colonized world, Nova Mars, she stumbles onto a ruin left by the original inhabitants. Her vampiric behavior dates from the discovery of a red jewel in the ruins. After years of drinking blood and sometimes killing, she meets a man she cannot and does not need to kill. Jace, brother of one of her victims, reveals to Sabella that she is actually an alien who, years in the past, took over the dying child Sabella's form and memories. Yet, because all the girl's thoughts and feelings live in this new form, the vampire *is,* in a sense, Sabella. Jace reassures her that, while neither Martian nor human, she is in some way both. Thanks to him, she learns to live without killing and to accept her past without self-destructive guilt. Jace reveals that he, too, found the Martian ruins in childhood and became absorbed into an alien being. He alone can safely nourish her, for they evolved that relationship in their former life as Martian lovers. Sabella speculates on how this relationship may have worked in the distant past, when Nova Mars was an inhabited but dying planet: "Of the little water and little food there was, one would eat and drink, and when he was strong, the other would take from him the vital element which food and drink had made--his blood... A system that requires a careful pairing, a creation of partners, who could permit in love what could never be permitted in hate or greed" (155). Learning this symbiotic relationship, learning to share in love rather than seize in greed, Sabella avoids succumbing to despair. Nor does she scorn and fear (as Professor Weyland in Suzy McKee Charnas' *The Vampire Tapestry* does) the elements humanity has contributed to her wholeness. Both the human and alien facets of her nature finally carry a positive connotation.

Her hard-won self-knowledge contrasts with the layers upon layers of illusion in Lee's novella "Bite-Me-Not or, Fleur de Feu" (1984). A tribe of winged vampires besieges a castle, where every facet of life is shaped by fear of the monsters; the color red is banned, blood is never seen, and the quest for the magical plant that repels vampires, the "flower of fire", obsesses the Duke. When the vampire Prince Feroluce breaks into the castle and is wounded in drinking from one of the Duke's caged lions, he is framed as "one of Satan's night-demons" (597), falling under the expertise of priests, sorcerers, and alchemists, condemned to death at sunrise. The scullery maid Rohise, illegitimate daughter of the Duke, interprets Feroluce through the songs of courtly love she has overheard. Re-visioning him from "monster or a monstrous beast" into "part of the dream-come-true" (601), she rescues him, fleeing with him as he flies back to the mountains. His people reject him as already dead. The pair, sharing no common language, dwell together as exiles. Feroluce conceives of the girl as a pet, no different from a wolf or eagle, but certainly not kin to the "human things" that captured him (608). When she offers her blood to him, he realizes that she is sentient and cannot serve as either "pet" or "prey"; at that point he "starts to see her as beautiful, not in the way a man beholds a woman," but analogous to a natural object, "the sheen of water in dusk, or flight, or song" (608). In the absence of rational communication, only "strange feeling or emotion, instinct or ritual" unites them, but above all they are bound "because they are doomed" (609). Since Rohise conceives of love in poetic terms, as an irrational attachment that demands extravagant self-sacrifice, she wholeheartedly accepts their shared fate. She absorbs his world-view, shunning the sun and fire as he does. Living wild in mountain caves, she becomes "an animal now, or a bird", forgetting that she was ever anything but "the essential mate" to Feroluce (610). When the two fly together over distant villages, their cries of ecstasy are "taken for the shrieks of malign invisible devils" (610). The omniscient narrator drily summarizes the consequences of union between human and monster: "There are always misunderstandings" (610). Unlike Sabella, who matures into a self-actualized hybrid of alien and human, Feroluce and Rohise lose their essential natures and dissolve into phantoms of legend, their only relic (reminiscent of Robinson's "Last of the Vampires") a "heap of peculiar bones, like parts of eagles mingled with those of a woman and a man", from which grows the mythical *fleur de feu* (612).

Sabella's solution cannot be generalized, since it depends on her union with Jace, the one living person who can serve as her symbiote. Auerbach numbers Sabella, along with Charnas' Weyland, among "superior beings whose lives the mortal reader is too ensnared to emulate" (147). Moreover, Sabella's relationship with Jace entails his dominating her, at least temporarily, until with his help she will learn "a discipline beyond myself" (156). This male-dominant image is balanced, however, by Sabella's foretaste of a future in which she will decide when and where to procreate the children who will revive their species. She also conceives an ecological vision, in which her offspring may revitalize the planet that she now sees as "a vampire too, taking from the life that moves over it, waiting for its resurrection from the deadness of a desert" (156). As Gordon puts it, creatures such as Sabella "come of age as vampires, mature morally, when they how learn to survive without killing" (233). Destruction of one's prey proves to be a primitive phase in a vampire's evolution, ecologically unsound and ultimately self-destructive.

A vampire dwelling in a Terran colony on Mars comes to terms with his relationship to humanity in *Nightshade* (1989), by Jack Butler. The narrative maintains an ambiguity about the nature of the vampire, John Shade, whether an undead human being or a member of another species who, like Martin's Joshua, considers himself human until his first "death". The novel's expository epilogue, however, attributes vampirism to a "data-storage mutation" (267). Scientists speculate that vampires can "store copies of themselves in some realm other than the biological, perhaps in a continuum something like the science fictional notion of hyperspace, or in the realm of pure information"; the drinking of blood, perhaps, functions as "an attempt to store the germ plasm, the blueprint of the race, safe from what harm might come" (267). Vampires, therefore, far from mere parasites, facilitate humanity's survival. It is further theorized that "the vampire mutation had been superseded by the creation of artificial intelligence" (267). Whatever his origins or purpose within the web of life, Shade, at any rate, stands apart from the human species. Yet he is not completely detached from humanity, for whenever he takes a victim's blood, it "changes" and "colors" him, causing him temporarily to absorb part of the prey's personality (162). Moreover, he unintentionally becomes a hero to his fellow citizens on Mars. Entangled in a revolutionary plot, he forms an alliance with an AI (a self-aware robot) and a female jangler (illegally created cyborg). The three of them, different from each other as well as exiled from the dominant culture, discover a mutual kinship. Jennie, the jangler, suggests that they are "x-people...X for unknown"; Mandrake, the AI, corrects her with the premise, "Y is farther out than X" (72). Shade, the vampire, proposes "a new dimension", concluding that "z is the farthest, the end" (72). They decide to call themselves "z-people, the androids from Planet Z. The z-oids," abbreviated as "zoids" (72). Reinventing themselves as "zoids", Shade and his friends create a community of their own to offset their alienation from the human community.

A distinguished example of an evolutionary perspective on the nonhuman vampire appears in Suzy McKee Charnas' *The Vampire Tapestry* (1980), featuring a vampire who periodically reinvents himself to ensure his survival. In addition, Charnas uses the alien vampire, in part, to deconstruct *Dracula* and its literary descendants. She makes her vampire a sympathetic character, not by romanticizing or sentimentalizing him, but by portraying him as an intelligent animal with his own place in our planet's ecology, simply trying to survive. She remarks in an interview that *The Vampire Tapestry* "came pretty much straight from *Dracula,* rebounding as it were--reacting against" (Carter, 4). She conceived her character, Dr. Weyland, as "an evolutionary product with a past reaching back into paleolithic times", in deliberate opposition to the stereotyped literary vampire, "a historical human with puffed up social pretensions", ultimately "based in this or that ethnic superstition complex" (4). In the first of the five sections of *The Vampire Tapestry,* Weyland, teaching as an anthropologist at a small college, delivers a lecture entitled "The Ancient Mind at Work" (also the title of the section, originally published as a novella in *Omni*). Toying with his audience, he answers the question, "Now, how would nature design a vampire?" (25). All his ostensible speculations about the "corporeal vampire...the greatest of all predators, living as he would off the top of the food chain" (25), are, of course, accurate descriptions of his own biology. He makes a point of dissociating the naturally evolved vampire from the traditional product of superstition and romance. He refers with scorn to the "blood-sipping phantom who cringes from a clove of garlic" (25), a "strolling corpse with an aversion to crosses" (28). The corporeal vampire does not sleep in a coffin or transform his victims into the undead.

Weyland dismisses the Byronic associations of the literary vampire as no less silly than the peasant superstitions. When a young woman in the audience suggests that the vampire, as a solitary predator, would be lonely, Weyland replies, "Predators in nature do not indulge in the sort of romantic mooning that humans impute to them" (29). When asked about the vampire's "Satanic pride"--another obvious allusion to Count Dracula--he sardonically remarks that "a tiger who falls asleep in a jungle and on waking finds a thriving city overgrowing his lair has no energy to spare for displays of Satanic pride" (30). (He refers here to the "long sleep" of suspended animation that carries him safely from one era to another when the present becomes too hazardous.) He responds to a comment about the vampire's erotic allure with the cold retort, "You are mixing up dinner with sex" (28). Weyland himself, the sole survivor of his species, remembers no childhood or parents and has never met another vampire. He has no erotic interest in human beings, engaging in sexual intercourse with his victims only as a form of protective camouflage.

How, then, does the author make this rationalized vampire, who regards human beings as livestock, attractive to the reader? The narrative structure of the novel itself engages the reader's sympathy. In the first section we see Weyland from the outside, as a dangerous predator, through the eyes of a woman who recognizes him for what he is and attempts to kill him. Each succeeding phase of the story, however, admits us further into the vampire's mind. The teenage boy protagonist of the second part, "The Land of Lost Content", meets Weyland, wounded and imprisoned, as the victim of a sadistic Satanist who wants to use the vampire to enhance his own power. Next we share the viewpoint of Weyland's psychologist, Floria Landauer, to whom he reveals his true nature, in the process discovering hitherto unsuspected truths about himself. Through this narrative structure the vampire, as Judith E. Johnson remarks, "shifts in and out of alterity", sometimes the "predatory Other" and sometimes the "attractive other" (79). The two final sections of *The Vampire Tapestry* enter directly into Weyland's consciousness, the last one narrated entirely from his viewpoint. By this point we no longer see Weyland as a monster, but as an intelligent creature surviving on his own terms. The vampire is revealed as "a sort of leftover saber-tooth tiger prowling the pavements, a truly endangered species" (31), an image that appeals to our ecology-conscious culture. As Auerbach notes, Charnas portrays the vampire as an animal at a period when animals function symbolically as "reminders of lost integrity" (150). Moreover, the novel contrasts Weyland's relatively modest predation--he drains small amounts of blood and avoids killing whenever possible--with the damage human beings inflict on their own kind. As Senf puts it, in fiction such as this, "ordinary human behavior" is revealed as "both frightening and cruel"; the vampire, as "an oppressed outsider who is frightened by this ordinary behavior, thus becomes less horrifying by comparison" (6).

The Vampire Tapestry presents a thorough and explicit analysis of the vampire as efficient super-predator, with multifarious implications for cross-species as well as human relationships. Human beings are simply "the vampire's livestock", no more significant to him than cattle are to us (25). Since in preindustrial times the vampire cannot travel far to find a fresh pool of unwary victims, he must periodically withdraw into extended hibernation: "A sleep several generations long would provide him with an untouched, ignorant population in the same location. He must be able to slow his metabolism, to induce in himself naturally a state of suspended animation" (26). Weyland suggests that this suspended animation, along with "minimal feeding", may contribute to the vampire's longevity, as research has shown to be the case with some animal species (26). The vampire's evolution favors long life over prolific breeding, for "the great predator would not wish to sire his own rivals" (26). Rather than using fangs to draw blood, the natural vampire (as in Polish folklore) has "some sort of puncturing device, perhaps a needle in the tongue like a sting that would secrete an anticlotting device" (26); therefore the vampire need not endanger himself by leaving conspicuous wounds or killing his prey with copious blood loss. This vampire is not only the supreme predator but the supremely adaptive animal: "It may be that he responds to the stimuli in the environment by growing in his body as well as in his mind. Perhaps while awake his entire being exists at an intense level of inner activity and change" (28). In modern times, of course, as the complexity of human society and the rate of technological advance constantly increase, the vampire must adapt faster and more radically than ever before. In Gordon's terms, he is primarily a "super-survivor".

This Darwinian perspective dominates the novel. David J. Skal notes the importance of evolutionary themes in *Dracula,* which he reads as, in part, "an anxious refutation or even a parody of Darwinian theory" (*V Is for Vampire,* 71). The late Victorian vampire's "blurring of the distinctions between humans and lower species", graphically symbolized by the scene in which Count Dracula "reverses the evolutionary process, descending the wall of his castle, crawling stealthily toward all our baser instincts and animal desires", evokes "horror" from the human protagonists (71). *The Vampire Tapestry,* in contrast, frames the kinship between *Homo sapiens* and other life-forms as largely positive. Weyland continually compares himself, and is compared by others, to animals. In the last moments before he relinquishes his Weyland identity to the long sleep, he looks forward to the future when he may "rise restored, eyes once more as bright and unreflective as a hawk's and heart as ruthless as a leopard's" (294). The one member of his lecture audience who knows his true nature reflects that the other spectators perceive "nothing of his menace, only the beauty of his quick hawk-glance and his panther-playfulness" (28). Mark, the teenage viewpoint character of "The Land of Lost Content", finds a painful reminder of Weyland's plight in a film of a coyote caught in a trap. Auerbach notes that Mark's generation "knows animals only as endangered species" (150). Simultaneously, the dualistic perspective that sets humanity in opposition to "beast" and "vampire" is deconstructed by frequent reminders that *Homo sapiens* also belongs to the animal kingdom. To Weyland, we are merely livestock and food. Commenting on human ecological wastefulness, Charnas says, "I just decided that there would be something that preyed specifically on *us*, but in a much more rational manner than we prey on the rest of the world, putting us (I wish) to shame for our moronic clumsiness" (Carter, 5; Charnas' emphasis). The result is Weyland, a creature with intelligence surpassing ours but with "the inner emotional life of the average housecat, a fact by the way of which he is well aware" (5).

This awareness lures Weyland into a vulnerable position. Not inclined to introspection, and having no others of his own species with whom to compare himself, he turns to a human listener as a mirror in which to contemplate his own nature. He stands out as one of the few solitary alien vampires (along with others such as Miriam in Whitley Strieber's *The Hunger,* Tanith Lee's Sabella, and the young vampire in Bob Leman's "The Pilgrimage of Clifford M.") to be considered in this study. Whether solitary or part of a vampire subculture, the various alien vampires in contemporary fiction each deal in slightly different ways with the human majority among whom they must live. One characteristic many of them share, however, is an impulse toward self-disclosure. Like Rice's Louis and Lestat, they want to justify themselves to the human world. Weyland goes to a psychologist, originally to get a certification of mental health to retain his professorship after his unexplained disappearance (a result of being shot by a vampire-hunter, a housekeeper at the college where he teaches). Against his conscious will, he finds himself revealing his true nature in therapy. The psychologist, Flora, remarks to Weyland that "beneath your various facades your true self suffers; like all true selves, it wants, needs to be honored as real and valuable through acceptance by another" (160). Similarly, Joshua in *Fevre Dream* tells his life story to Abner Marsh. On this unprecedented occasion, vampires and human "cattle" speak and listen honestly to each other. Accepting the risk of "sharpened stakes", Joshua communicates with Marsh in hopes of "a true partnership"; Marsh responds, "I never lissened to no vampire before neither, so we're even... This here bull is lissenin'" (144). Bob Leman's Clifford, a vampire brought up by human foster parents, knowing nothing of his own heritage beyond what he can deduce from legend and ambiguous news reports of mysterious assaults, leaves a final message to his human allies before he commits suicide in despair at what he has discovered about his true nature.

The creatures of the night, in turn, attract human beings for a variety of reasons. Weyland fears that scientists in search of "the inner secret" would in the end deal with him as ruthlessly as those dominated by "lust for power" (86). Dissecting him to hunt for answers "in the brain, the heart, the gut, the bones", the "curious men" of science "would be as cruel as the mob" (87). As a victim of the human lust for power, Weyland becomes the target of Alan Reese, a Satanist who strives for self-aggrandizement by dominating the "demonic" vampire; yet Reese also reveals a suppressed desire to become a vampire himself. When Weyland, helpless from a nearly fatal gunshot wound, becomes a prisoner in an opportunistic New Yorker's apartment, his "host's" friend Reese arranges private exhibitions of the "monster" for his fellow cultists, to "display the antagonist he means to subdue" (92). Weyland explains to his captor's teenage nephew, "In reality, I can give Reese nothing--but he can take from me. He 'builds me up'...in order to stand higher himself when he has cast me down. He presents me as some mystical and powerful being which he alone, the leader, the master, can conquer and destroy" (92). As in Siebers' theory of superstition, Reese uses the exclusion of Weyland as a "demon" to enhance his own status. But at the novel's climax, when Reese tracks Weyland to his new home in Albuquerque, it turns out that appropriating the vampire's power by subduing him is no longer enough for Reese. Reese projects his own concept of power, his "dream of secret superiority" (286), upon the alien. Recognizing this subliminal motive, Weyland encourages it with seductive remarks such as, "I know that even in your childhood something cruel lived in you, not simple childish brutality but a core of ice for the sake of which you held yourself aloof" (286). Having studied the dreams and myths of his prey, Weyland recognizes and evokes in Reese the archetypes of a child raised by wolves who "becomes the leader of a mythic pack ranging the forest forever" or a misfit who is told by a messenger from the stars, "Come, you are not one of these wretched little mammals, this has all been a mistake. You are one of us, mighty, wise, and immortal" (286). Once the Satanist's guard has been breached by the awakening of his desire to become what he ostensibly hates, Weyland manages to destroy him. Like Weyland's near-fatal shooting at the hands of Katje in "The Ancient Mind at Work", his confrontation with Reese illustrates how, in Marleen Barr's words, "Charnas eradicates the definite distinctions between 'creature' and 'human', 'hero' and 'villain', 'hunter' and 'hunted'" (70).

Other people project their own emotions upon the vampire in more benign, though no less distorted, ways. A female student at Weyland's lecture about the vampire as supreme predator asks, "Wouldn't he be lonely?" with "her posture eloquent of the desire to comfort that loneliness" (29)--an overture that Weyland scorns. After the lecture, Katje, the woman who later shoots Weyland in self-defense, muses, "For overcivilized people to experience the approach of such a predator as sexually attractive was not strange" (31). Weyland reflects that Alison, a graduate student who serves him only as "a food source to be cultivated", never actually sees him, "but rather the fatherly part I played" (249). Only Floria, his therapist, recognizes what he is and is drawn to him because of his otherness, not in spite of it. She realizes that because her work as a psychologist is "designed to make humans more human", she may be endangering his essential selfhood (161). If vampirism is indeed "the core of his identity", she must not use her therapeutic skills "to cure him of what he is" (153). In *Vampire Dreams*, Charnas' dramatic adaptation of this part of the novel, Weyland explicitly charges Floria with trying to "inflict your rituals upon me in hopes of turning me into what you are" (40). Auerbach maintains that in the play the "unprofessional embrace" between therapist and vampire proves "unequivocally destructive", rather than, as in the novel, ambiguous (215). Whether the word "destructive" is appropriate, certainly Floria in the dramatized version functions as the primary catalyst in Weyland's decision to retreat into his deathlike sleep, whereas in the novel she acts as only one of several influences bringing about his unwanted transformation; moreover, in the play she herself appears more deeply and permanently changed than in the book, forced, like Weyland, to abandon her established life and reinvent herself.

In contrast to the many guilt-ridden vampires of popular fiction who long to be "cured", Weyland, rather than wishing to become human, views the prospect with repugnance. Yet living in the midst of human society inexorably alters him. Since he has to pose as a human being to hunt his prey (a necessity he resents), he faces the danger of becoming what he imitates. He tells Floria, "The seductiveness, the distraction of our--human contact worries me. I fear for the ruthlessness that keeps me alive" (161). One symptom of his growing similarity to his victims is his love for ballet, a quirk he finds puzzling; why should he be emotionally stirred by the creations of inferior beings? At a production of *Tosca* in Santa Fe, the opera moves him so violently that it throws him into a temporary fugue, a reenactment of a moment from an earlier lifetime. Afterward, he speculates, "Where did it come from, this perilous new pattern of recognizing aspects of himself in the creations of his human livestock?... Had he been somehow irrevocably opened to the power of their art? He recoiled violently from such possibilities; he wanted nothing more from them than that which he already, relentlessly required: their blood" (226). Weyland, however, cannot turn back and renounce what he has gained; only the long sleep can obliterate his unwanted awareness. He speculates that he has worked through this process many times before, in his forgotten past lives. One purpose of his extended coma, he suspects, is to free him from the weight of unmanageable awareness and unbearable memories. Despite his resistance to the process, he does reveal his true self to Floria and finds the experience valuable. In a letter written to her but never sent, he says of their single sexual encounter, "Perhaps I desired, there at the last, to repossess a part of myself I had unwittingly given you. At other times I think I wanted to touch a part of you that our speaking together had revealed to me" (252). In the end, though, he refuses the invitation to become human. He sees himself as "afflicted [not blessed] by attachment" (293), when he realizes he has begun to care for some of his human associates. "His life had been broken into, anyone might enter" (293). He even comes to understand (though he still hates the man) the drives and needs of his enemy, Reese. As Gordon suggests, "the vampire's sentience makes him aware of the suffering of his prey, and of its existence not just as a species but as an individual. Such awareness is a kind of love" (232). Recognizing the threat such "love" poses to his identity as a predator, Weyland resolves, "I am not the monster who falls in love and is destroyed by his human feelings. I am the monster who stays true" (293).

Despite the hazard of revealing themselves to their prey, many alien vampires in fiction yearn to reach out to human companions as strongly as the human characters yearn for knowledge of the alien other. And despite the reluctance of some, such as Weyland, to admit any kinship between themselves and their victims, the vampires' situation throws light upon aspects of the human condition. Weyland considers his similarity to the human race, including his sexuality, to be no more than "detailed biological mimicry, a form of protective coloration" (138). Commenting on human ambition, he distances himself from such motives by emphasizing his own simplicity: "And people think of a vampire as arrogant!... This one wants to be President or Class Monitor or Department Chairman or Union Boss, another must be first to fly to the stars or to transplant the human brain, and on and on. As for me, I wish only to satisfy my appetite in peace" (157). Floria reflects on a former (human) patient whom she restored to functional health, only to have him go on to establish "a hellish 'home' for the aged" and "destroy the helpless for profit", a memory that makes her realize, "W. not my first predator, only most honest and direct" (158). The contrast between a vampire's modest depredations and the horrible behavior of human beings toward their own kind forms a recurrent theme in recent vampire fiction.

Just as Weyland has an objective view of human ambitions and conflicts, he has a similar detached perspective upon human sexual customs. He casually cuts to the heart of the traditional position of women, stating that he finds men more accessible as prey "because women have been walled away like prizes or so physically impoverished by repeated childbearing as to be unhealthy prey for me" (132). With no erotic interest in human beings, either male or female, he prefers to hunt homosexual men because their fringe position in society makes them vulnerable. When a fellow professor introduces him to a lesbian couple, Weyland reflects, "Whether a person slept with partners of one sex or the other was one of those distinctions humans invented and then treated as a tablet of the law" (268). Maureen King reads this statement as a message of tolerance, a subversion of "the insistence in the more conventional vampire narrative upon heterosexual relationships which maintain a system of male domination and female submission" (81). While this element may be present at some level, I regard the remark mainly as an illustration of Weyland's detachment from humanity and his emotional incomprehension of the nuances of human sexuality, which he studies only in order to manipulate potential food sources. He certainly displays no empathy for homosexuals as fellow outcasts; as noted above, he pragmatically chooses gay men as victims because their marginal status gives him an advantage. In general, he views sex (aside from the act of mutual disclosure with Floria) as "little different from conversation and other forms of social falsehood", tools for use in snaring prey (251). When he watches a man and woman dancing together in the ballet, he interprets their interaction in terms of "hunter" and "prey" (155). Floria observes, "W. isn't man, isn't woman, yet the drama connects" (155). Anne Cranny-Francis reads *The Vampire Tapestry* in part as identifying woman with monster, both of them marginalized and victimized, with Weyland embodying "the empathic monster, the woman-identified subjectivity" (173). Weyland seems to me, rather, to transcend conventional masculine-feminine roles, as Floria's remark illustrates; his occasional vulnerability does not render him feminine any more than his stereotypically "fatherly" behavior with Alison renders him masculine. As a nonhuman creature wearing a human mask, he deconstructs what King refers to as "the binary oppositions--such as good/evil, human/alien, and masculine/feminine" (75).

Despite his own lack of interest in sex and nonconformity to socially conditioned gender roles, Weyland proves erotically attractive to female characters within the novel. For instance, Floria finds herself drawn to him because as a result of "the single, stark, primary condition: he is a predator who subsists on human blood", he possesses "[h]armony, strength, clarity, magnificence--all from that basic animal integrity" (160). Her own life, by contrast, seems disordered. Through her interaction with Weyland she regains her focus, while he becomes open to human attachment in a new way--and finds the depth of his unwanted caring for his human associates frightening. Floria, as Weyland recognizes, is attracted by his essential alienness. He puts her desire, as he perceives it, into words: "As to the unicorn, out of your own legends--'Unicorn, come lay your head in my lap while the hunters close in. You are a wonder, and for love of wonder I will tame you'" (161). He fears the "distraction of...human contact" and tells her, "I fear for the ruthlessness that keeps me alive"; he dreads becoming a "predator paralyzed by an unwanted empathy with his prey...fit only for a cage and keeper" (161). Recognizing this danger, Floria makes it clear that she does not wish to reform, dominate, or exploit Weyland. When, upon their final meeting, they share sexual intimacy for the first and only time, she embraces the experience of "unlike closing with unlike across whatever likeness may be found" (178).

Miriam, the solitary vampire of Whitley Strieber's *The Hunger* (1981), responds to the human fascination with the Other by a reciprocal fascination. Like Weyland, she is (as far as we know in this novel) the last survivor of her species, though, unlike him, she remembers others of her kind. Like Weyland, she, too, suffers the indignity of imprisonment by human beings--in her case, medical researchers probing for the secret of her immortality--who wish to use her, in a reversal of the vampire-victim roles. Miriam's attitude toward her prey, however, contrasts with Weyland's contempt for the human race. While he scorns the "romantic" notion of the vampire's loneliness, Miriam "was lonely, and human beings gave her the love that pets give" (Strieber, 64). Weyland wants nothing from his prey but their blood and resents even that much dependence on them; Miriam, on the other hand, takes one human companion after another, obsessed with futile attempts to transform her victims into creatures like herself. Despite the temporary illusion of success, these attempts always fail. Miriam sees her fascination with humanity, self-centered though it is, as a form of love. She attributes the decline of her species to the dangerous seductiveness of humankind: "If one loved human beings, how could one also kill them and still be happy enough with oneself to love one's own kind, and bear young?" (189). Unlike Martin's Joshua, she remains incapable, despite centuries of experience, of forging a healthy relationship with a member of our race. She enjoys sexual liaisons with human partners and, like most vampires, exercises erotic magnetism over both men and women. In *The Hunger* she becomes attached to a brilliant young scientist, Sarah, whose research holds the promise of transmitting Miriam's immortality to ordinary people. Once again Miriam's hopes are crushed, however, and at the end of the novel she takes a new lover, knowing she will "dream her dream of his immortality and tell herself that here at last was her eternal companion" (246). But she also knows that in time "nature would come and shatter her dream" (246). She has at last learned her lesson: "No matter how her loneliness tempted her to find one who would last forever, she resolved never to attempt the transformation of another Sarah, not this time or the next time, or for all time" (246). In Miriam's world the attraction between human and alien proves deadly to both. As Auerbach puts it, "the triumph of vampirism is the failure of sharing" (59).

Another alien vampire destroyed by his inability to become fully human appears in "The Pilgrimage of Clifford M." (1984), by Bob Leman. Unlike Weyland, though, Clifford craves humanity. Accidentally stolen from his parents and brought up as human, Clifford (like Martin's Joshua) does not fully recognize his alien nature until he reaches maturity. Ironically, he has less chance of fitting into the human world than any other alien vampire in fiction. His kind begin life as voracious, den-dwelling carnivores with fur and shark-like teeth, growing after a decades-long childhood into outwardly human but completely nocturnal creatures feeding solely on blood. When Clifford realizes his biology is too radically different for him to be a variant of *Homo sapiens*, he undertakes a search for his origins. He wins the reader's sympathy through his loneliness and his quest for self-knowledge. Though a savage beast in childhood, Clifford outgrows this phase and, once educated, leads the life of a wealthy, reclusive scholar, feeding circumspectly without killing or seriously harming his prey.

Finally, with the help of a group of human investigators, he discovers what are probably the last three living vampires in North America, two of them his own parents. He finds that with age, adult vampires become nearly mindless predators. This story, even more than *The Vampire Tapestry*, explicitly deconstructs Dracula. Unable to face his future as foreshadowed in his vampire relatives, Clifford leaves a suicide letter directing his human allies to kill him along with the other three. He dresses for the occasion in a tuxedo and opera cape, wryly amused by the prospect of resembling Count Dracula at the moment of his death. Led astray by popular fiction, he realizes he had visualized vampires as "cultivated humans who possessed--as it happened--certain nocturnal proclivities, and who required a somewhat specialized diet" (Leman, 30). Instead he finds "dangerous and disgusting vermin" and realizes, "It would be quite impossible for me to live among such creatures; I would rather live with hyenas" (Leman, 30). He has acquired his erroneous notions about his own species from human cultural stereotypes. Anticipating his own inevitable degeneration, he falls into despair. In explaining his suicidal choice to his human allies, Clifford, like Weyland speaking honestly to his therapist (or, for that matter, Anne Rice's Louis and Lestat breaking the taboo against revealing themselves to the mortal world), enacts the impulse toward self-revelation seen in many contemporary fictional vampires. Just as we wish to understand these not-quite-human creatures, they long to be understood.

Leman's protagonist has no desire to transform human beings into vampires; instead, he originally thinks of himself as human. Besides the compelling desire to know his true nature, another motive for his quest is "simple lust; but lust for whom, for what? Not any woman that he had ever met; not any man or child or beast. This most urgent drive was toward a female of his own kind" (Leman, 18). Therefore cross-species eroticism plays no part in Leman's story; unlike Miriam, he cannot achieve emotional connection with humanity through sexual intimacy. When he discovers members of his own species "diurnally lying comatose in a muddy burrow, awakening only to prey disgustingly upon human beings" (27), his quest ends in disillusionment. Since he cannot stomach the thought of mating with the female, his sexual and social isolation becomes complete. His well-meaning foster parents and teachers, unwittingly attempting to make an alien into a human being, have instead rendered him unfit for either world. He explains in his written *apologia,* "I was born a creature not human, and inhuman I am; but I was reared as a human, and human I am in my thoughts and attitudes...I would like to be human" (29). The vampire becomes a symbol for any member of a minority group who loses his own identity but cannot be assimilated into the dominant culture. As Clifford realizes, "I cannot be a human being. I will not live as what I am" (30). Portraying Clifford as the ultimate outsider, Leman, like Strieber, shows human-alien interaction as destructive.

The narrator of Jody Scott's *I, Vampire* (1984) appears to have come to terms with her outsider status. Scott's vampire, as Veronica Hollinger says, "is the subject of her own story rather than the object of another's and the interpreter of events rather than the event interpreted" (11). The improbably named Sterling O'Blivion, seven hundred years old, descends from a French-Irish family living in Sibiu, a Transylvanian city associated with Vlad the Impaler. In the twentieth century she works at a dance studio in Chicago. Extraterrestrials visit Earth, and Sterling falls in love with one of the shapeshifting aliens, disguised in the form of Virginia Woolf. The novel thus deconstructs gender and species distinctions. As, in Hollinger's words, "a victim of the kind of binary thinking that defines the Other as evil", Sterling subverts "the oppositional barriers between human and Other" (11). Scott's vampire displays an uncommon degree of self-respect, even as a teenage girl afflicted with "that unspeakable 'it'--the defective gene" that makes her a vampire (1). This "radically wrong" trait, loathsome and terrifying to her family and neighbors, seems to her "minor, natural, and even quite pleasant" (1). When her parents disown her as demonic, she feels "terribly unhappy about no longer being loved, but not a bit guilty" (3). God, after all, has created her with the need for blood, and those who persecute her are "the cruel ones" (3). Sterling's requirement for "six ounces of human arterial blood once a month" is "not an ethical choice. I was born this way" (13). In demystifying the vampire's predation, the text foregrounds, instead, human violence. In Sterling's eyes, ordinary human beings "have an elitist attitude about themselves. They can do any horror they like to other species, but when it comes to their own persons that's a different matter" (12-13). The interstellar invaders, the Rysemians, endorse Sterling's judgment; they are prepared to exterminate the human species if humanity cannot evolve beyond its present lethal behavior patterns. This novel, according to Hollinger, "effects a satiric inversion of the conventional alien-invasion plot, since it is humanity which is cast as the dangerous life-form in the narrative" (12). The Rysemians, ironically, choose as their ally the "monster" who lives on human blood.

"A Winter's Night" (1988), a novella by P. H MacEwen, also frames the human race as irresponsibly destructive, in need of direction from a superior being. Elliston, the story's vampire narrator, reluctantly initiates survival-motivated interaction with a family that has survived a global war. Nuclear winter confers the benefit of perpetual night upon the solitary vampire, as he searches for potential prey, finally discovering a man, a woman, and two children hiding in a potato cellar in Idaho. Structured in epistolary form, alternating Elliston's journal with the woman's letters to her dead sister, the little girl's diary, and the man's calendar notes, the narrative contrasts the vampire's covert oversight of his human charges with their desperation and their dim awareness of Elliston's presence. The woman reacts to his nocturnal visit with sexual arousal and thinks of him as "ghost lover" (124). The man, when he sees Elliston and another vampire face to face, identifies them as "Brujo things" with "demon eyes" and "wolf teeth with yellow knives" (131-132). The vampire, in turn, regards the people as "cattle", protecting them as a herdsman would care for livestock (129). Upon encountering another of his race, Elliston kills the other vampire to protect his human "proteges" (124). Unlike other vampires discussed in this chapter, Elliston has no desire to communicate with the lesser beings under his care, not even to correct their superstitious misconceptions about him. He dreams of "a renewed human race and a rebuilt civilization...this time in ignorance of us, yet under our guidance, our dominion" (130). Without letting the survivors know of his manipulation, he directs them to a new home in a Civil Defense shelter stocked with food, medicines, and other supplies. Meanwhile he refrains from feeding on them, not from ethical motives, but in the spirit of a conservationist. The text's images of human-created devastation imply that *Homo sapiens* has failed to take proper care of the planet and therefore deserves to be treated as livestock under the control of a superior race. While *The Vampire Tapestry* conveys its message of humanity's wasteful destructiveness by portraying the vampire as an animal in danger of extinction, MacEwen's story, thematically similar, assigns that role to our own species.

The fiction of Elaine Bergstrom features aliens (of extraterrestrial origin, but of such long-term residence on Earth that they consider this planet their home) who, though clearly superior to *Homo sapiens,* respect humanity. Like Elliston, but sometimes from altruistic motives, they secretly watch over human proteges. Like other more or less benign fictional vampires, Bergstrom's vampire clan, the Austras, balance their predation with service to the host species; moreover, their weaknesses--particularly their reproductive difficulties--offset their superhuman powers. Not only do they take blood from human prey (as well as lower animals), they also need the human race to revitalize their own gene pool. Similar to Petrey's Varkela females, who often die at puberty, Austra females usually die in childbirth. Helen, the human-alien hybrid of *Shattered Glass* (1989), her vampire nature awakened by blood-sharing with Stephen Austra, offers the promise of birth without inevitable sacrifice of the mother. Symbiotes rather than parasites, the Austras also contribute to humanity's long-term welfare through the products of their genius under the cover of their corporation, AustraGlass, whose creations in stained glass have adorned human architecture since the Middle Ages. Just as their empathic connection to their prey, discussed below, compensates for the blood they drink, their contributions to human culture balance (if not atone for) the killings they have committed over the centuries. At their best, the Austras achieve a wholeness unavailable to isolated characters such as Weyland, Miriam, or Clifford.

Bergstrom's vampires exert an irresistible magnetism over human beings, an involuntary phenomenon that operates, especially when the vampires hunger for blood, unless they consciously suppress it. Also, because (like many fictional vampires) they possess telepathy, they can shape their behavior to satisfy the human partner's inmost desires. In *Shattered Glass* the first victim of the renegade, homicidal vampire, Stephen's brother Charles, finds that he pleasures her "[p]erfectly--as she would herself" (Bergstrom, 3). Under his touch, "a passion such as she had never known began to build in her... Her fears, her needs, her life were forgotten as she shuddered in a fulfillment of glorious intensity" (3). While some of these creatures, such as Charles, lapse into feeding upon terror and pain, positive emotions constitute their more usual nourishment. As Stephen's brother, Charles functions as his double and shadow (the two look enough alike to be mistaken for each other), the "evil" vampire, defined by his disregard for human life, in opposition to the "good" vampire, defined by his positive connection to humanity. Beyond sexual union, the Austras use telepathy to satisfy the human yearning to know the Other. Stephen says of a woman he has touched only briefly, in search of information, "we were closer than most lovers will ever hope to be...she let me touch old wounds" (267). Like Lichtenberg's luren and Petrey's Varkela, the Austras fulfill in fantasy the otherwise unattainable wish to plumb the depths of another's mind. While drinking a human donor's blood (and sometimes without blood-sharing), the vampire can share his or her memories with the donor in a reenactment so vivid it seems actually to be happening.

On the individual level, the Austras seldom relate to human associates as equals (although selected human associates, such as the employees of AustraGlass, enjoy the family's protection). Their own kind always come first in their priorities; as Charles reminds Stephen, "sacrifice is not a usual family trait" (361). Charles begs absolution from a priest, but only for offenses committed against members of his family; he feels no guilt for killing human beings. "I feed on you but you are nothing to me," he says, much as Weyland might; "You are not my kind" (313). Stephen, whose love for Helen provides the text's bridge between alien and human, nevertheless cautions Helen's uncle, Dick Wells, "Caring is a luxury. Do not expect me to be indiscriminate" (262). Dick sees the vampire as an "alien bastard" (304), yet eventually comes to accept the Other's standards as valid from an alien viewpoint. Stephen reminds his human friends of "eras when those of my blood were hunted and destroyed for what we were and, more often, what we were thought to be" (280). As in *The Vampire Tapestry,* where Weyland fears the invasive curiosity of science no less than the superstitious lynch mob, Stephen recognizes the horror of "the plans your modern world would have for us if it knew of our existence" (280). He fears being used as "a piece of mental artillery in [humanity's] endless conflicts" and feels certain that as inhuman creatures, his kind would have "no rights, if that is convenient" (280). Again, the most dangerous threat comes not from the alien predator, but from the human beings who, given the chance, would exterminate the Other as a monster. When Stephen chides himself, "You're getting too human...too rational" (23), he refers to the risk of loving Helen and accepting her family's friendship, but the text may also imply an ironic reference to the hazard of embracing the darker side of human nature, for "love of power--the kind of power humanity so delights in wielding" is, according to Stephen, a "vice" that his people "dare not claim" (280).

Nancy A. Collins constructs a different kind of interface between vampirism and humanity in *Sunglasses After Dark* (1989). Sonja Blue, the vampire protagonist of the series beginning with this novel, shares her identity with two other personae, Denise Thorne, her original, mortal self, and the Other, the embodiment of demonic bloodlust. As Sonja, drained and abandoned by the vampire lord Morgan, she becomes a vengeful vampire-hunter, companion to Ghilardi, a mad would-be Van Helsing who teaches her the arcane lore of the world into which she has been forcibly initiated. Meanwhile, the Other taunts her with remarks such as, "What makes the word 'human' so damned wonderful? You're always mourning your humanity, denying yourself the power and privilege that are yours by right for fear of becoming inhuman" (152). Urging her to give up her habit of drinking bottled blood purchased on the black market and instead to drain a mugger who has tried to murder her, the Other demands, "Who's the monster, Sonja? You or him?" (152). The "evil" wrought by a lost young woman transformed without her awareness or consent pales beside the crimes of humanity. Mundane human evil is epitomized by Catherine Wheele, a greedy evangelist with psychic energy-draining powers comparable to Sonja's own. Catherine has chosen to use her talent "to bilk sick and deluded humans", a squandering of resources "like using a laser to engrave postcards" (234). Pangloss, one of the elder vampires Sonja discovers, maintains that "no atrocity mankind has perpetrated on itself" has been engineered by the nonhumans among us (140). At the same time, the "supernatural" beings are far from benign. Pangloss views human beings as "myopic little beasts intent on destroying their world" (139). He wishes to prevent this destruction only in the spirit of a "farmer" refusing to "stand idly by and watch his herd die of hoof-and-mouth" (140).

Ghilardi, Sonja's mentor, calls these powerful beings "Pretenders", because "they pretend to be human, hiding their demonic *otherness* behind a mask of carefully constructed banality" (111, Collins' emphasis). Yet, ironically, their realm is also referred to as the Real World, a dimension to which ordinary human beings are blind and deaf: "The Pretenders dwell in the cracks in mankind's perception of reality" (110). Humanity knows these creatures-- "vampires, werewolves, incubi and succubi, ogres, undines, and demons too numerous to mention"--only through "myth and legend, twisted beyond recognition" (111). All these entities, like the menacing Other in countless paranoid fantasies, "can pass for humans, and they prey on them" (111). A vampire, in Collins' system, comes to birth when a victim dies after exposure to the saliva or sperm of a vampire. After death, "the corpse undergoes radical physical and genetic restructuring," a transformation completed when "a minor demon enters the host" (111). Because this entity "has no frame of reference, only raw instinct", it constructs a personality for itself using "the only thing on hand: the brain of the victim" as its "template" (111). The process resembles the possession and transmutation that converts Lee's Sabella from human child into alien vampire. Unlike the typical vampire, Sonja experiences transformation without actually dying; hence she grows into her powers with abnormal rapidity, and the "Denise Thorne" self is not quite dead. This abnormality may account for the ethical scruples that enable her, at first, to resist the bloodlust of the Other. As the Other's personality encroaches on what she thinks of as her true self, it grows from "constant companion" and "silent, parasitic partner, feeding on...emotions" into Sonja's "intangible Siamese twin, joined at the medulla oblongata" (115). Throughout the novel she wrestles with questions of humanity and identity, finally coming to terms with both Denise Thorne (through her residual entanglement with Catherine Wheele and Denise's father, Jacob Thorne) and the inescapable Other. Like Sabella, Sonja acknowledges her ties with her former, human life, while confronting the truth that she has changed into something alien.

Love between alien and human plays a prominent role in many of these works, such as *Those of My Blood* and *Shattered Glass*. It is not surprising that some authors have made the love story central to their work, giving rise to a distinct subgenre of vampire romance. While not a conventional romance, Tanith Lee's *Dark Dance* (1992), first book of the Scarabae trilogy, begins like a formulaic Gothic novel, with the orphaned Rachaela summoned to the isolated mansion of her father's peculiar family. There she meets her long-lost father, Adamus, who looks no more than thirty years old. Repeating the pattern of his single night with Rachaela's mother, Adamus mates with Rachaela only until she becomes pregnant. Their child, Ruth, matures with abnormal speed and grows, of course, into a vampire. In the ravishingly attractive, hypersexual Adamus, Lee crafts a nightmare parody of the tender, passionate, Byronic vampire lover of conventional romance. He cares nothing for Rachaela except in terms of her fitness to bear the "Scarabae seed" (94); he plans to breed with their daughter Ruth as soon as she reaches the age of fertility. Rachaela visualizes the Scarabae as animals, "wild things dwelling in a stained-glass forest" (57). They present themselves to her as a persecuted clan, subject to "pogroms" (46), a term that associates them with ostracized ethnic minorities. Rachaela feels no attachment to or sympathy for them, nor does she feel anything for Adamus beyond erotic attraction mingled with bitter resentment. The baby Ruth is a "thing" to her, "horrible and inhuman", a parasite that has used her body (236). She imagines Ruth wearing a sign around her neck: "Conceived from my father while he drank my blood, suspected of being a demon" (246).

The more typical demon-lover romances involving alien vampires portray their male protagonists (the vampire in such stories is almost always male, the human partner female) as ultimately benign. If their race tends toward callously predatory behavior, the hero is an exception, committed to moral responsibility, often as a result of his love for the heroine. Jasmine Cresswell's *Prince of the Night* (1995), set in Italy in the 1850s, centers upon Count Dakon, a member of an extraterrestrial species stranded on Earth, who can mate with human females but always produce male offspring. He displays his high ethical standards by avoiding women of breeding age, because even if a human female survives copulation with a male vampire, she is likely to die in childbirth. In addition, Dakon risks his life for his human neighbors as a freedom fighter in the service of the Italian revolution. Like *Dark Dance, Prince of the Night* follows the general pattern of Gothic fiction, with heroine Cordelia Hope a reluctant guest at the Count's estate, the Villa of the Three Fountains, and entangled in the mystery of the villa's reclusive lord. Cordelia, of course, proves to be uniquely suited to mate with Dakon, since she has the ability to respond to his telepathic overtures. He tries to stay away from her, despite the agony of resisting the mating drive. Only Cordelia's determination forces him to take the risk of union with her.

Nicholas, the nonhuman hero of Sue Krinard's *Prince of Dreams* (1995), is a psychic vampire, feeding on the energy of dreams. His extrasensory power makes possible a deeply erotic intimacy with the heroine, Diana. Fearful of draining her energy to a harmful or fatal degree, he carefully ensures that the dream embraces they share have only a positive effect on her. Like Stephen in *Shattered Glass,* Nicholas is opposed by his brother, Adrian, a thoroughly destructive energy-vampire who disdains Nicholas' scruples about repaying human donors with comfort and peace. After Adrian's death, Nicholas, burdened by loneliness as the last of his kind--a rare instance of an alien vampire who longs for a "cure"--attains mortality through Diana's love.

In each of these novels, despite the heroine's independence and strong will, the hero's alien abilities produce an unequal power relationship between them. Because the male belongs to a superior species (emphasized by the word "Prince" in the novels' titles), the pairing conforms to the traditional romance model of dominant, protective male and protected, rescued female. What subverts this model, in each case, is the restoration of balance provided by the vampire's need for his human beloved, for more than nourishment. Cresswell's Dakon needs Cordelia not only for the telepathic intimacy that fills his emotional emptiness, but, more fundamentally, as the mother of his child and therefore the instrument of his family's survival. Unlike Lee's Adamus, Dakon consummates the union with a human bride out of love, not impersonal instinct. Cordelia, miraculously, bears the first girl infant fathered by a vampire on our planet. (As in *Shattered Glass,* the text makes no attempt to rationalize the biological details of crossbreeding between inhabitants of different worlds.) In Diana, Krinard's Nicholas finds love, an end to loneliness, and thereby mortality--forfeiting his nonhuman immortality for deliverance from the pain of being the last of his race. She also delivers Nicholas from the guilt he suffers because of his need to drain energy from unsuspecting mortals; he fears his kind have become extinct because they "were never meant to live on this earth" and were an "affront against nature" (423). Diana reassures him, and through the strength of her love makes him believe, that his people have repaid humanity by using dreams to inspire "great artists and thinkers" through the ages (423). Reconciliation, essential to the romance genre, is achieved in these novels through the merging of the best elements in both human and alien, a union symbolized by the marriage of hero and heroine.

A more recent series, by Christine Feehan, likewise foregrounds the strengths of union between different species. Beginning with *Dark Prince* (1999), yet another novel whose title frames the vampire race as aristocracy, Feehan's series introduces the "Carpathians". Only the renegades among them, ruled by bloodlust, are labeled "vampires", and the key to resisting the darkness within lies in finding one's destined life mate. In *Dark Prince,* Mikhail, head of the clan, dominates human heroine Raven by his psychic powers as well as drinking her blood and seducing her into sexual intimacy. At the same time, she exercises reciprocal power over him by virtue of her status as his soulmate. Conflict arises not only from within the Carpathian clan, but also from the now-familiar trope of fanatical, religiously motivated vampire hunters blind to the fact that "monsters" may be free-willed individuals, some of whom behave with ethical responsibility. Raven, in contrast, remains open to Mikhail's fine qualities despite her indignation over his arrogant, headstrong treatment of her. The image of finding fulfillment in mating with a uniquely destined Other whose very survival depends on that bond has a powerful appeal. On the other hand, the "life mate" or "soulmate" concept lies open to the charge of postulating an inexorable destiny that the heroine (not to mention the vampire hero himself) cannot escape, hardly an empowering premise. Nevertheless, the theme of a healing synthesis between male and female, human and nonhuman, and the characters' bestial and spiritual selves does dominate Feehan's romance series.

Similarly, in Steven Spruill's *Rulers of Darkness* (1995), "hemophage" Merrick Chapman finds his strength in love for an intelligent, independent woman, forensic hematologist Katherine O'Keefe. This novel also uses the "good vampire/evil vampire" model to dramatize Merrick's ethical standards in contrast to Zane, Merrick's own son, selfish, violent, and purely survival-driven. Because Merrick cares for Katherine, he renounces her in order to avoid hurting her by staying young and deathless while she ages. Her determination to love him brings them together again, and they seek a cure for Merrick's immortality and blood-need, so that they can live out their lives together. Meanwhile, factors in Merrick's blood offer the promise of extended life and health for ordinary mortals. Though a suspense novel rather than a formulaic romance, *Rulers of Darkness* also focuses on the reconciliation between human and nonhuman attainable through intimacy between the sexes.

That reconciliation between species is less prominent in J. R. Ward's Black Dagger Brotherhood paranormal romance series. Her characters differ from the typical vampires of folklore and fiction in that human blood does not constitute their primary diet. While they can consume it, human blood is an inadequate substitute for what they need to survive, the blood of a member of the opposite sex of their own species. Thus, Ward establishes a strong link between sexuality and blood-need. These vampires do not remain completely aloof from humanity, however. Interbreeding between the two populations sometimes occurs, and Wrath, the hero of *Dark Lover* (2005), the first novel in the series, falls in love with a human-vampire hybrid heroine. Ward's vampires live for about a thousand years and undergo "transition" to adulthood in their mid-twenties, when they lose the ability to endure sunlight, and at that time both sexual desire and the need for the blood of the opposite sex awaken. Ward embeds her characters in a complex mythology involving two quasi-divine figures, the Scribe Virgin (creator of the vampire race) and the Omega (eternal enemy of the Scribe Virgin and her creations), as well as the Lessening Society, a cult of soulless, formerly human servants of the Omega dedicated to exterminating vampires (called "the lesser", they have been rendered ageless and can be killed only by stabbing through the heart). The elite Black Dagger Brotherhood, led by Wrath, protects their own kind from the hunters of the Lessening Society. Under the terms of this mythos, it would be possible for vampires to live entirely on the fringes of human society. In practice, phenomena such as the possibility of fosterage with human surrogate parents (as in the case of Wrath), occasional bonding with a human mate, and, as mentioned above, the existence of crossbreeds prevent that kind of total detachment.

At the opposite extreme, the Ina, the vampires of Octavia Butler's *Fledgling* (2005), live in intimate symbiosis with human blood donors. Although they have their own origin myths, the Ina do not actually know whether they came from another planet or evolved alongside humanity on Earth. They cannot breed with Homo sapiens; however, they depend on human symbionts not only for blood but for emotional connection. These vampires' venom is intoxicating and addictive, so that once bonded, their symbionts, of which each

Ina has a household full to avoid draining any one individual, cannot leave their Ina or even want to. In addition to the intense pleasure of giving blood and sometimes sharing sexual passion with the Ina, they also gain the advantage of improved healing and extension of their lifespan to a couple of centuries. Shori, the first-person narrator, looks like a child, even though she is really over fifty years old (still childhood for her species). At the beginning of the novel she has lost her memory in the aftermath of a brutal attack that destroyed her home and killed everyone in it except her, both Ina and human. A young man driving by picks her up and quickly becomes enthralled by her. Gradually she discovers her true nature, connects with other Ina clans, gathers a new group of symbionts, and searches for the murderers of her family. She learns she is targeted for assassination because she is the product of a genetic experiment in adding melanin to vampires' bodies through insertion of human DNA, in order to make them less sensitive to the sun. Although the Ina do not disintegrate or burst into flame in sunlight, they are terribly vulnerable to its damaging effects.

The genetic engineering performed on Shori makes her dark-skinned, infusing the text with racial implications. Her family was murdered by hostile Ina who consider her an abomination, framing the racism in this novel as an intra-species conflict rather than pitting the human and vampire populations against each other. Wright, the young man who becomes Shori's symbiont, observes that the human members of an Ina household seem happy with their lot. He questions, however, whether their apparent happiness can be authentic when addiction to the experience of donating blood undermines their free will. Another potentially disturbing issue in this novel is the apparent age difference between Wright and Shori. Although her chronological age surpasses his, she has the physical aspect of a preadolescent girl. Therefore, the erotic attraction between the two of them carries overtones of pedophilia, even though Shori exercises the power in their relationship. Thus Butler explores racism, power relations, sexuality, and the nature of love through the figures of the Ina and their human dependents. As Shawn Taylor points out in *Parables, Vampires, and Pregnant Men* (2017), *Fledgling* destabilizes and interrogates the predominant tropes of vampire fiction, with its most high-profile examples in popular culture foregrounding white males in positions of power.

Members of the *Homo sapiens nocturnus* subspecies in S. M. Stirling's Shadowspawn trilogy, beginning with *A Taint in the Blood* (2010), also possess human dependents, but on rather different terms from the Ina and their symbionts. The Shadowspawn derive their obvious inspiration from Williamson's classic *Darker Than You Think*. In fact, at one point the dialogue alludes to Williamson (although not by name) as a New Mexico writer who stumbled upon part of the truth, wrote a book about it, and was nevertheless permitted to live into his nineties. Like *Homo lycanthropus*, the Shadowspawn embody the truth behind the legends of werewolves, vampires, witches, demons, incubi, and cruel gods who demand human sacrifice. Myths and fairy tales worldwide preserve ancestral memories of the prehistoric Empire of Shadow. As in *Darker Than You Think*, the creatures can leave their bodies and, while incorporeal, wear different shapes. They can twist probability to perform feats that look like magic to ordinary mortals. At death, if they successfully "transition", they become permanently incorporeal and much more powerful than in the "birth body". Silver hurts them, and sunlight and nuclear radiation have deadly effects on the incorporeal form. Stirling updates the concept with references to DNA and quantum entanglement. For instance, in order to assume the astral form of another animal or person, his vampires must ingest material containing the DNA of the chosen subject. They have immense power to control human minds and manipulate the target's perception of reality, including the ability to "carry" the psyche of a victim within their own mental landscape, indistinguishable in all sensory respects from the material world, somewhat like the monsters in Kim Newman's *Bad Dreams* (to be discussed in the next chapter). The Shadowspawn can even extend this captivity beyond the subject's physical death, granting a nightmarish sort of immortality. The vampiric dimension of their nature is more prominently displayed than in Williamson's version, with *Homo sapiens nocturnus* frequently indulging in the consumption of human blood. Moreover, they require blood to fuel "Wreaking", the exercise of their psychic abilities. In the process of Wreaking, they sometimes speak a sinister, ancient tongue called Mhabrogast, which is either the native language of Hell, the operating code of the universe, or both.

Their sociopathic level of sadism and their reluctance, as solitary predators, to trust each other place the main limits on their power. Only the residual human component in their genetic makeup enables them to work together at all. They control the world, but covertly rather than openly. Despite their preternatural powers, they are on average no more intelligent than ordinary people; in fact, reliance on their psychic gifts tends to make them mentally lazy as well as arrogant. Like Williamson's monsters, Stirling's vampiric beings have bred with their human prey over the millennia, so near-purebloods are rare, and many members of the general population have some measure of the vampires' psychic ability. This heritage depends on the percentage of Shadowspawn genes, ranging from a simple predilection for reliable "hunches" to psychic powers that approach those of true Shadowspawn. Both the vilest tyrants and the holiest saints tend to have high proportions of *Homo sapiens nocturnus* genes, the latter reacting against their predatory instincts. Individuals who fall in the middle of the continuum, with enough Shadowspawn traits to crave blood but not enough to gain nourishment from it, become deranged serial killers. Some people willingly come to an accommodation with the monsters and embrace the roles of "renfields" (servants and assistants) and "lucies" (blood donors). Lucies are bound to their masters or mistresses by a blend of fear, addiction, and sometimes adoration, while renfields serve from a variety of motives, from the purely mercenary to a sense of obligation, as with one character whom her Shadowspawn patroness cured of terminal cancer.

Adrian, the hero, and his cruel sister Adrienne (who resembles a tiger with human intelligence) are among the few near-purebloods, having a higher percentage of Shadowspawn genes than anyone previously born since the fall of the Empire of Shadow. Their twin children (conceived several years before *A Taint in the Blood* by Adrienne's incestuous rape of Adrian) are, of course, even less human, but the second and third volumes of the trilogy strongly imply that, under Adrian's care, they may grow up valuing humanity as he does. As part of her ongoing love-hate obsession with her brother, Adrienne kidnaps Adrian's human lover, Ellen, who until that night has no idea of his true nature. Adrian has broken away from his species' bloodthirsty lifestyle and is trying to live as nearly as possible like an ordinary human man. He corresponds to Williamson's "Dark Messiah", except that Adrian, unlike Will, is fully aware of his background. He works with his old friend and mentor from the Brotherhood, a secret organization fighting against the Shadowspawn. Most of its members, ironically, carry a higher than average proportion of *nocturnus* genes and use the resulting psychic abilities to protect ordinary humanity. In the process of Adrian's rescue of Ellen, the couple gets entangled in the Brotherhood's fight against a long-term plot to reduce Earth's overpopulation (as the Shadowspawn see it) and restore the vampire-shapeshifter-sorcerers' open rule over humanity. Adrian remains recognizable as a dangerous, inhuman predator even while he struggles against his darker urges. Unlike Williamson, Stirling does not imply that the Shadowspawn "taint" is the wellspring of all human evil. Anyone, regardless of his or her genes, has free will to behave ethically or not, as demonstrated by Adrian's choice to live as a "good" monster.

Fortitude, the protagonist of *Generation V* by M. L. Brennan (2013), strenuously but ineffectively strives to reject his biological heritage in favor of leading a quasi-human existence. Fort has a college degree in an impractical major, a job at a coffee shop, an unfaithful girlfriend, and an obnoxious roommate. Unlike most stereotypical Gen X bachelors coping with their first experiences of "real life", however, he belongs to a family of vampires. Not having yet made the "transition" to adult vampirism, he is still mostly human. Fort detests his need to drink blood from his mother at regular intervals and puts it off as long as possible. Because, contrary to custom, he was brought up until the age of nine by human foster parents, he also clings to human attitudes baffling to his mother and two siblings, Chivalry (brother, who has a human wife he truly loves) and Prudence (sister, the most sociopathic member of the family). These vampires become biologically more inhuman with increasing age, e.g. in prominence of fangs and intolerance for sunlight and solid foods. In this species, both males and females have functioning genitalia but lack the capability to reproduce. Instead, they must create "hosts" through a blood-exchange process that changes the human victim's physiology so radically that offspring conceived by him or her have vampire DNA. Creating a viable host is a difficult procedure few vampires succeed in accomplishing. Madeline, Fort's mother, is highly unusual in having managed to create two hosts, male and female. Unfortunately, the process has negative effects on the human subjects, eventually reducing them to an animalistic, uncontrollably violent condition. Near the beginning of the novel, a vampire from a different territory arrives to pay his respects to Madeline. When he turns out to be a homicidal pedophile, Fort becomes determined to rescue the villain's one surviving abductee, a little girl. Fort's family members refuse to help with what they see as an irrational mission that violates vampire etiquette. Like many works of fiction belonging to the urban fantasy subgenre, Brennan's series complicates the protagonist's situation by involving representatives of other monstrous species, such as Suzume, a kitsune hired by Madeline as a bodyguard for Fort. In dealing with various nonhuman allies and antagonists as well as coping with his transition to full adulthood, Fort repeatedly finds both his principles and his competence tested. *Generation V* and its sequels comprise a bracing blend of suspense, humor, character growth, and ethical quandaries.

The dissolution of barriers between human and nonhuman also forms the central theme in several late twentieth-century juvenile and young adult novels, a rapidly growing subdivision of the vampire fiction field. Two series, in particular, merit notice. A group of novels for elementary school children, "Fifth Grade Monsters" by Mel Gilden, features a cast of characters clearly defined as members of other races or subspecies, not transformed human beings. One of these is a vampire child eager to fit into the mainstream culture of a grade school classroom. Gilden evokes sympathy for "monsters" by drawing a parallel between these creatures and outcast, persecuted human minorities. The series constantly emphasizes (often with didactic explicitness) the value of accepting people who look different, perhaps at first sight even threatening. In the opening volume, *M Is for Monster* (1987), human protagonist Danny discovers that the four monster children who join his fifth-grade class--Howie Wolfner, an English werewolf; Frankie and Elisa Stein, German twins who wear bolts in their necks and generate electricity from their bodies; and C. D. Bitesky, a Transylvanian immigrant who wears evening clothes with a cape to school and carries a thermos of red liquid called Fluid of Life--make far better friends than Stevie, the *human* class bully. The bigoted Stevie tries to discredit the "freaks", while Danny and other sympathetic characters accept them and try to understand their differences. Though Danny has some initial problems overcoming the stereotypes he has absorbed from horror movies, the obvious friendliness of the "monsters" quickly changes his attitude. Elisa suggests that "what you call a monster is all in your head" (34), while C. D. reminds Danny, "We are your friends... Does it matter where we come from or what sort of blood is in our veins?" (34). Drawing an implicit analogy with the mainstreaming of the physically challenged, Elisa compares monsters to "people with special problems--or special abilities" (34). Thus at the outset Gilden establishes a metaphorical equivalence between vampires and two formerly stigmatized populations, ethnic minorities and the disabled. C. D.'s name obviously suggests "Count Dracula", and the series makes several references to his famous relative, "The Count". But despite the horror traditionally associated with the name "Dracula", C. D. and his family are harmless, drinking Fluid of Life rather than feeding on live prey. Gilden's novels place them on the side of the oppressed rather than (like Stoker's Dracula) the oppressors; the Biteskys have fled old-country persecution in search of a better life in Brooklyn.

In *How to Be a Vampire in One Easy Lesson* (1990), the Count himself takes refuge in Brooklyn for that same reason, making his home in the cellar of a grand old movie house, the Carfax Theater. (Its name is one of many allusions to Stoker, directed to adult rather than child readers; for example, the theater's owner, Abby Carfax, drives a van that she nicknames Helsing.) A benefit screening of Bela Lugosi's *Dracula* at the theater leads to a discussion of horror movies, which C. D. and his monster friends dislike because "they perpetuate a negative stereotype" (7), a lighthearted allusion to similar consciousness-raising among human minority groups. Stevie, fascinated by the film, decides he wants to become a vampire, not because he has undergone a conversion from bigotry to tolerance, but because he wants to appropriate the monsters' power. He wants to become a more efficient bully by dominating others with the force of his will (perhaps analogous to Caucasians who try to appropriate Oriental and Native American modes of spirituality with impure motives and imperfect understanding). Though C. D.'s parents introduce Stevie to the Count, this selfishly motivated attempt at transformation naturally fails. C. D.'s family, as non-supernatural creatures, cannot transmit their powers to ordinary people. After Stevie realizes his "change" is a delusion, C. D. reminds him, "Before we began I told you that you are a vampire or you are not... It is like having red hair and freckles" (90). Gilden's vampires, rather than undead revenants spawned by the Devil, are simply a subgroup of humanity, to be accepted on their own merits as individuals, not stigmatized *en masse* as "monsters". The text's choice of "red hair and freckles" as an analogy emphasizes the relative superficiality of the differences between C. D.'s kind and "normal" children.

Ann Hodgman's *There's a Batwing in My Lunchbox* (1988), the one book in the series not written by Gilden, uses the monster children to foreground the importance of pride in one's own ancestral heritage. C. D. proves to be the only student with the courage to speak up when the fifth-grade teacher, Ms. Cosgrove, plans a traditional Thanksgiving feast. The vampire boy refuses to participate, because his forebears had no connection with the Pilgrims, and turkey and pumpkin pie hold no cultural resonance for him. To his surprise, children of other ethnic backgrounds speak up to support him. Only Stevie, expressing his usual bigotry against the monsters, accuses C. D. of being "a complete unpatriot" (9) and threatens to have his father report C. D.'s rebellion to the school board. Ms. Cosgrove, recognizing her own ethnocentrism, decides instead to have a multicultural feast, with each student bringing a family recipe from his or her ancestral home, to "celebrate *all* the immigrants who have come to this country" (29, Hodgman's emphasis). Howie the werewolf underscores the analogy between monsters and more mundane persecuted minorities with the remark, "The Pilgrims would probably have run *my* ancestors out of town--or burned them at the stake" (13, Hodgman's emphasis). When C. D. presents his contribution to the Thanksgiving feast, a Potion of Friendliness, he tells the class that "my family has been persecuted there [Transylvania] for centuries... In America, in England, in Transylvania--perhaps all over the world--no one likes people who are different" (64). The identification of vampires (and other victims of superstition) with human outsiders could hardly be more explicit.

Young adult fiction, while also foregrounding the plight of traditionally marginalized groups and calling into question definitions of "human" and "monstrous", additionally uses vampirism to explore adolescent concerns about identity, the maturation process, and separation from parents. In *Secret Vampire* (1996), the first volume of L. J. Smith's "Night World" series, the transitional phase of adolescence represents a radical discontinuity between childhood and adulthood, symbolized by transformation into a vampire. Although Smith's teenage protagonist, Poppy, is forever cut off from her old status as her parents' child, she achieves a new level of maturity and manages to integrate the vampire and human facets of her life. Before the discovery that she will die of pancreatic cancer within a month, she has "two great ambitions"--"to see the world" and to marry her long-time friend, James Rasmussen (5). Both of these naive ambitions receive grimly ironic fulfillment; she "marries" James through the sharing of blood, and as a new vampire, she has no choice but to travel, since she cannot let her parents and friends know she still lives.

Wholesome and well-adjusted though she is, Poppy displays some traces of rebellion in her desire for autonomy, wishing she had a mother like James' laissez-faire parents, instead of her own, "always worrying and trying to fix" her (11). James enjoys enviable freedom, living in his own apartment as manager for a building owned by his parents. Poppy also expresses her drive toward independence by choosing as her best friend the "tough and dangerous" James, whom the other girls think of as "a mysterious, secretive bad boy", whose "vulnerable, caring side" only Poppy can see (17). She alone recognizes his "differentness" and imagines that if he ever told her his secret, it would be "as shocking and lovely as having a stray cat speak to her" (12). James, in fact, belongs to a separate species, a vampire race living alongside humanity as part of the Night World, the realm of vampires, werewolves, shapeshifters, and witches. The law of the Night World forbids allowing humanity to learn of the nonhuman races' existence and, above all, forbids falling in love with a human being. To vampires--"lamia"--and the other folk of the Night World, ordinary people are "vermin" (31). James' cousin Ash regards him as "a little soft on vermin" (186) and harboring "radical permissive ideas about humans having free will" (187).

Given his psychic bond with Poppy, however, James risks capital punishment to save her life. The malignant tumor itself is described in vampiric terms, a "pain...gnawing deep inside her" (45). James' kind of vampirism, in contrast, appears benign and life-affirming. He has "canines like a cat's", silver eyes, superhuman speed and strength, and preternaturally acute senses (51). Like Weyland, he is compared in positive terms to natural predators. His kind normally feed without killing, using their hypnotic powers to induce forgetfulness. Explaining the truth about his race, James tells Poppy, "Everything you know is wrong"; her misconceptions about vampires are "picked up from books or TV" (54). Despite their long friendship, her prejudices against vampires are not easily overcome. That her "best friend is a bloodsucking monster" is as great a shock as the realization of her own imminent death (55). Although he may be "some godawful undead fiend", he offers her only hope for life (57). Her use of the term "undead" demonstrates that she has not yet assimilated what James has told her. The choice he offers threatens the core of her identity; she protests, "I'm *me*. I can't be--like that" (56, Smith's emphasis). When she allows him to change her into a vampire (the mechanism, given his status as a member of a separate species, is not explained), she literally dies to her old life and begins a new one. She discovers in the act of blood-sharing a "sensation of release, of giving", in which she and James grow "closer and closer, like two drops of water moving together until they merged" (60). Their telepathic communion makes the drinking of blood into a form of symbiosis, a symbol of the ultimate intimacy. They are "not predator and prey, but partners in a dance" (61). She regards vampirism as "part of Nature" and "a way of giving life, pure life" (118). On the night of the third and last exchange of blood, which initiates Poppy's mock death, she feels as if the occasion is "some terribly important birthday and graduation rolled into one"--a rite of passage to another plane of existence (77).

Human-vampire prejudice operates in both directions. Vampire lore teaches that the intimacy shared by Poppy and James is abnormal, that he should feel only "the joy of the hunt" (80). To prevent his parents from learning that he has transformed Poppy, James must pretend indifference to her death, mouthing the Night World creed that "they aren't really *people*" and that losing a human friend is "sort of like losing a pet" (94, Smith's emphasis). Poppy's brother Philip, to whom James must reveal the secret of her survival, responds with typical human revulsion, "I could never figure out why you gave me the creeps" (99). James realizes that Philip now considers him "less than human" (99). He protests, "I'm not some bug-eyed monster from Alpha Centauri", but Philip continues to react like "a junior space captain talking to the alien invaders in a B movie" (100). To Philip, James is "unnatural" and "wrong", something that "shouldn't exist" (101). Attempting to move the discussion onto a rational plane, James advances the ecological argument that his kind are simply "higher up on the food chain" than *Homo sapiens* and do only what they "have to do to survive" (101). Only when he fully realizes that James offers Poppy's only hope does Philip begin to overcome his prejudices. Even as he helps James with Poppy's transition, he struggles with mental images of "Poppy as a Hollywood monster. Red eyes, chalky skin, and dripping teeth" (150). Gradually he abandons his popular culture stereotypes of vampirism and accepts that Poppy, although transformed into an inhuman creature "with the eyes of a jaguar" (158), has made a valid choice. Traditional vampire fiction in the *Dracula* pattern portrays the vampiric metamorphosis as defilement and damnation. To Poppy, vampirism is, rather, a "part of Nature". As Auerbach remarks (in reference to the film *Love at First Bite*), the contemporary romantic vampire is "no loveless leech...but a restorer of lost powers and a deliverer into new spaces" (166).

Smith's text foregrounds the absolute break between old and new selves symbolized by Poppy's "death" and resurrection. She feels "like a snake shedding its skin, to reveal a fresh new body underneath" (159). She asks herself, "Have I turned into something awful?" and concludes that she is "just different. Not awful" (167). Upon telephoning her old home to hear her mother's voice, she suffers "a dizzy Twilight Zone feeling" and comes to terms with the fact that she is irrevocably exiled from that home (181). She has "lost her family and her old life and maybe her childhood" but "found herself" (171). Her new self is explicitly eroticized, making vampirism a metaphor for sexual maturation. She no longer looks like "something that sits on a buttercup", but rather, "wild and dangerous and exotic" like a "model" or "rock star", with "silvery-green, uncanny" eyes (170). The awareness of her change afflicts her with momentary terror. She chides herself, "So what did you expect to look like, Shirley Temple?" (170). Predator though she has become, she achieves acceptance of her new identity without killing or exploiting human beings. At the conclusion of the novel, in a fairy-tale "real princess" denouement, Poppy and Philip discover that their latent clairvoyant talents arise from witch ancestry in their family background. Therefore they actually belong to the Night World, so that Poppy and James can declare their love openly among his kind. Philip, forced to accept his own nonhuman heritage, acknowledges that vampires may not be "as completely bad as they seem"; after all, they "don't treat their food any worse than humans do" (224). Poppy concludes that they need not be "horrible bloodsucking monsters" but perhaps "can be *decent* bloodsucking monsters" (225, Smith's emphasis). Philip, who chooses to retain his human lifestyle, serves as a bridge between his sister and the world she has renounced. Poppy completes the mature integration of the two halves of her nature by visiting her mother in a dream to bestow a measure of peace and acceptance.

The second "Night World" novel, *Daughters of Darkness* (1996), also explores human-vampire relationships but devotes more attention to the vampire viewpoint than the previous novel does. The text portrays mundane society through the eyes of three naive vampire sisters who flee from their lifelong home on a vampire-ruled island to a new life with their eccentric Aunt Opal. Like their brother Ash (James' cousin), they bear traditional vampire names--Rowan, Kestrel, and Jade--adopted from the natural world of plants, birds, animals, and precious stones, foregrounding their inhumanity. Kestrel's remark, "Free-range humans are so much better than kept ones" (16), makes their alien world-view obvious from the beginning. Their naivete about the outside world is clear in Rowan's frightened plea for reassurance that vampire hunters "aren't real", but "just stories to frighten kids" (24). When they find Aunt Opal's desiccated body transfixed by a stake, the sisters must deal with the murder and its legal consequences as any teenagers in the same predicament might, but with the added complication of their alien nature. As one of Ash's vampire friends remarks, because the sisters have spent their lives "on an island completely separated from normal humans", they have not learned "how cunning vermin can be" (35). These vampires view *Homo sapiens* as a cross between a dangerously intelligent prey animal and an inferior racial strain. Ash himself, something of a James Dean among vampire youths, finds Aunt Opal's choice to live isolated from her own race in a human town intriguing, a life with "no competition" and "no Elders putting a limit on how many you can bag" (33). Nevertheless, he shares the Night World contempt for ordinary people and those of his own kind foolish enough to become entangled with them. His model for sexual relationships mimics that of a promiscuous human adolescent, a preference for "shapeshifters with cute furry tails" and "human girls with fancy sports cars who never seemed to mind when he nibbled their necks" (83). When he discovers that he and human protagonist Mary-Lynnette are "soulmates", an "involuntary" state in which the two parties bound together may be "completely wrong...in every way--wrong species, wrong temperament, wrong age" (126), he reacts with horror. Unlike James and Poppy in their joyful acceptance of their soulmate status, Ash and Mary-Lynnette fight the bond they share.

Mary-Lynnette expresses her adolescent drive toward individuation through a love for astronomy. Her telescope and the stars it reveals to her represent her growing awareness of the universe beyond herself and her family. When she first looks into Ash's eyes, she interprets the shock of their connection as a vision of "galaxies gathered into clusters and superclusters, bigger and bigger, until size lost any meaning and she felt herself falling" (68). Ash's alien qualities both allure and frighten her. From the beginning, she senses his predatory, animal nature. When the electricity of the bond flashes between them, he looks to her "like a cat who's had a shock" (69). In the dark his eyes appear "all pupil. Like a cat's at maximum dilation" (88). Once she recovers from the revelation of what he and his sisters actually are, Mary-Lynnette rejoices in the discovery of someone who shares her love for the night. The experience also unsettles her concept of her own identity, however; she reflects, "I may not be who I've always thought I am" (92). The darkness, she fears, cannot be "any human's natural habitat" (93), yet she no longer fits into the familiar niche she has occupied for most of her life. Recognizing the three vampire sisters as not "malicious" but "practical" in the same sense as "a lioness or a wolf or a falcon", she faces Rowan as a fellow "alpha female" in defense of her younger brother (who has fallen in love with Jade) (110). Asking herself whether it is "worse to drink deer blood than to make baby cows into boots" (115), she enters a blood-bond with the three sisters. She sympathizes with their rebellion, their desire to "see the human world" and "to eat junk food...read magazines and wear pants and watch TV" (124). While Rowan, Kestrel, and Jade explore the outside world and the enticements of popular culture, Mary-Lynnette reluctantly acknowledges her bond with Ash and considers becoming a vampire. In Rowan she finds, for the first time, "a friend who was completely her equal, who found it as easy to take care of people as to be taken care of" (165). Mary-Lynnette comes to perceive Ash as "somebody who would accept her completely, who would share everything with her" (122).

Like many teenagers, she feels herself a misfit in her previously familiar world and longs for a friend or lover who can appreciate her unique self. She wants to "discover a supernova and study mini-quasars" and "be the one who solves the mystery of where all the dark matter in the universe is" (138). Her unasked-for bond with a vampire calls into question her still inchoate adult identity. After the first tentative blood-sharing with Ash, she sees herself as a "fierce" creature who will "enjoy running through the darkness, underneath stars as bright as miniature suns" (193). At the same time, she has strong misgivings about abandoning her family and her human life. Unlike Poppy, she is not forced into the vampire realm by the prospect of imminent death, and finally Mary-Lynnette chooses humanity. She, too, however, has passed through an irrevocable rite of passage. Having tasted vampire blood and witnessed violent death (of the werewolf responsible for Opal's murder), "she would never look in the mirror and see the same person she used to see" (215). Ash temporarily departs, but they do not deny the love flowering between them. Ash must consider whether he can endure being bound to a human partner and giving up the Night World; he must also reevaluate his past callous treatment of the human prey he has always regarded "as vermin--and food" (225). Whereas Poppy begins her new life dependent upon James, who has rescued her from certain death, Ash and Mary-Lynnette begin their relationship as equals. Each must make adjustments, and neither has to change his or her essential nature. Mary-Lynnette does not have to become a vampire to be worthy of Ash. She comes to terms with her true self, someone who will eventually "discover a supernova or a comet or a black hole, but...do it as a human" and will "always love the night" (228). This novel focuses, finally, upon overcoming the barriers between races, cultures, and species without violating the self-worth of any.

All these works pose questions of what it means to be human and what obligations human and nonhuman beings have toward each other. They deal in a variety of ways with the ethical problem faced by an intelligent, self-aware creature who requires the blood of other sentient beings for survival. Wilson's novel frames its aliens as fundamentally destructive, invaders with whom no alliance or compromise is possible. Carlsen, the protagonist, concludes that they cannot be trusted, a judgment the text appears to support. Collins' Pretenders also appear innately hostile to humanity, but individuals among them--at least one individual, the anomalous Sonja Blue--can overcome the demonic tendencies of the species and aspire to ethical behavior. Other works portray the alien as a free-willed being capable of moral choice, no more intrinsically "evil" (or "good") than humankind. Authors such as Bergstrom and Spruill dramatize the vampire's dual nature as irresistible predator and powerful ally through conflict between "good" and "evil" characters. The most optimistic vampire-as-alien novels reflect a positive vision of human relationships with other kinds of human beings and with nonhuman life. Bergstrom, Petrey, and Lichtenberg model mutual exchange and sharing between "our kind" and the alien. Charnas illustrates the importance of respecting the integrity and uniqueness of the Other, instead of trying to distort him or her into a copy of ourselves. As Lichtenberg suggests, these novels invite us "to step sideways into another universe and become another person for a while." In Tiptree's phrase, we are encouraged to "dream outwards". This exercise of entering the mind of the alien invites an analogy with our understanding, or lack thereof, for the real-world "other" sexes, races, and species who inhabit our own planet.

Chapter 4

On the Edge of the Herd
(Post-1980)

While interviewing Anne Rice, Michael Riley alludes to the dearth of human characters in her Vampire Chronicles, particularly their near-total absence from *Interview with the Vampire*. Riley remarks to Rice that in her "version of the myth viewers and readers perceive these characters, the vampires themselves, as human"; in *Interview* "the audience doesn't experience the absence of a human victim" because "the vampires *are* the human victims" (262, Riley's emphasis). Rice agrees that her vampire characters "are metaphors for us" (262). Nevertheless, the fact that these characters are portrayed as nonhuman predators inevitably makes a difference in the reader's perception of them and, therefore, of the world-view presented in the text. Auerbach reads the "segregation of vampires from mortal society" exemplified by Lestat and his ilk as "complicity in a restorative ideology that re-erects barriers", including those between "white Christians and alien Others" (186). If, as Auerbach says, the "interpenetrative" vampires of the early to mid-nineteenth century drew their power from "the response they aroused in mortals", the "clannish and self-enclosed" (186) creatures of contemporary vampire fiction often regard mortals as objects whose "response" as sentient beings is irrelevant to the vampire's needs. A character's distance from our kind is still more striking when that character is literally alien, not a former human being. In some alien vampire novels, even when a "human victim" not only occupies the foreground but serves as a viewpoint character, the text may place more emphasis on the inhumanity of the vampire than upon any potential for communication and connection between species. In *The Vampire Tapestry* Weyland's colleague Irv says of the human need for connection, "It's too cold and lonesome for us out beyond the edges of the human herd" (270). Weyland mentally denies any such need in his own kind: "Not for a lynx...that is his place" (270). Whether or not such detachment is indeed feasible for Weyland is problematic; however, some alien vampires in recent fiction seem ideally suited to life beyond the edges of the herd.

The nameless protagonist of "Halley's Passing" (1987), by Michael McDowell, carries the isolation ostensibly preferred by Weyland to extreme lengths. Like Weyland, McDowell's vampire is unique, the only one of his kind. The text represents his lack of personal identity by assigning him, in succession, the various false names he borrows from the licenses and credit cards of his victims. This character is all facade, with no substance. His entire existence consists of traveling from place to place, utilizing modern technology to the fullest in his endless hunt for prey. An obsessive recorder, like Stoker's characters--particularly Renfield with his columns of figures--McDowell's vampire writes all his travels and financial transactions in a black loose-leaf notebook. By keeping a written record of his activities instead of trusting to memory, he avoids establishing a pattern by which "a perfect pursuer", an imagined "nonexistent, dogged detective" might discern the connection among his murders and track him down (78). He has no other interests, "no other business" besides taking victims and evading capture, unresponsive to "any pleasure but that moment he saw the blood of each night's new friend" (81). Finding prey early in the night leaves him "with a long stretch of hours till he could sleep with the dawn"; if he puts off his nightly feeding, he spends "the long hours fretting" (81). He calls his victims "acquaintances", not only because "he simply had no other word for them", but also because "really, they were the people he got to know best" (78) --hence the ironic term "friend". His bloodlust has diminished to the tasting of a mere drop from each victim, the placing of "an incrimsoned finger to his lips", nothing but "a febrile memory of what had once been a hot true necessity of desire" (81). In short, this vampire not only lacks a fixed human identity, he is devoid of any substance in himself. His memory of his own past, much beyond the last century, fades into a blur. The orbit of Halley's Comet, growing fainter with each passage, symbolizes the weary cycle of the vampire's own life, drained of all purpose except feeding to survive another night to feed yet again. On a continuum of involvement with humanity, McDowell's vampire stands at one extreme, diametrically opposite to such characters as Bergstrom's Austras, Petrey's Varkela, and the romance heroes of Krinard and Cresswell.

The series beginning with Brian Lumley's *Necroscope* (1986) charts a complex web of relationships between its aliens, the Wamphyri, and the human race; in the first book, however, Lumley's vampires function as pure parasites and predators, with whom no compromise is possible. Set in the context of the Cold War, *Necroscope* centers upon the covert struggle between secret British and Soviet ESP intelligence-gathering agencies. On the British side, protagonist Harry Keogh is recruited for his talent of speaking with the dead, as the only known fully developed "necroscope". The chief antagonist, Boris Dragosani, is a necromancer, who dismembers corpses with his bare hands and teeth to rip out their secrets. The dead love Harry, especially the "great thinkers" who, after death, "go on thinking their special thoughts", creating works of artistic and scientific genius, "finishing all the unfinished thoughts they never had time for when they lived" (209). Harry provides a mind with which to share these thoughts, to relieve the loneliness of the afterlife. One of his dead friends explains the difference between the necroscope's talent and Dragosani's: To the dead, Harry is "bringer of warmth, of peace" and "contact with the dream that went before" (396); they communicate with him gladly. The necromancer, on the other hand, "reaches in and takes, steals", finding "answers in your blood, your guts, in the marrow of your very bones" (396). He tortures his lifeless victims, raping the truth from their remains. Dragosani, although physically an ordinary human being, behaves like a vampire; in a reversal of the traditional vampire-victim relationship, a living man preys on the dead.

Through Dragosani's greed for power, a nonhuman vampire forces its way out of its grave to renewed life. Already a psychic vampire of sorts, the necromancer, entrapped by the alien's wiles, eventually becomes a literal vampire. Dragosani first mistakes Thibor Ferenczy, the "thing in the ground" imprisoned by silver chains in its ruined tomb, the "old devil, the dragon" for an undead creature like the monsters of legend (153). Conversations with the vampire disabuse him of misconceptions about sunlight, crosses, mirrors, and running water. Dragosani's necromantic power has originated as a gift from Thibor, through an affinity born of the fact that Dragosani was conceived atop Thibor's grave, with a drop of his mother's blood nourishing the vampire. As Thibor's metaphorical child, Dragosani has communicated with the "thing in the ground" for most of his life, seduced by the vampire with promises of ever increasing power. To the last Thibor encourages Dragosani's self-deluded ambitions, allowing the necromancer the illusion of equality with the monster, while the vampire refers to himself as "just a poor undead Thing in the ground" (417). Only gradually does Dragosani learn the truth behind the vampire legend, that the former Wallachian prince is no longer human, not even a human revenant. The Wamphyri are nonhuman creatures that live within the bodies of human hosts, in a merging that Dragosani first perceives as symbiotic, but in fact constitutes a parasitic infiltration that takes over the host's entire being. This invasion, reminiscent of the vampiric possession in Wilson's *Space Vampires,* differs in that the Wamphyri's possession of a victim is always permanent.

Using an evolutionary perspective to justify his rapacious existence, Thibor reminds Dragosani that the "primal vampire was a thing of Nature no less than the primal man" (318). Not a "thing of darkness, loyal subject of Satan" (167), but a product of biological forces, the vampire dwells within its host as a lump of protoplasm like a "great leech" with a head like a cobra's (498), capable of manifesting itself as a "phallic tentacle", extruding a "pseudopod" with "barbs" used to attach itself to the victim's internal organs (431). Amorphous, the entity can form tentacles, eyestalks, manipulatory digits, teeth, whatever appendages it needs. Upon entering its victim, the parasite's "terrible tentacle did no real harm, no damage. Protoplasmic, it moulded itself to organs without crushing them, penetrating without puncturing" (432). Its substance intertwines itself throughout the host's body, down to "the individual whorls of [the victim's] brain" (414). To Dragosani's original--and foolish--wish to become a vampire, Thibor responds with deceptive evasions, whetting the young man's greed while clouding his mind: "I can no more explain how to be Wamphyr than a fish could explain how to be a fish... If you tried to be a fish you would drown" (165). Later, when it is too late to resist, Dragosani learns through painful experience that he can become a vampire only by receiving Thibor's egg, the "one spawning, one new life to move on down through the centuries" (415) allotted to each Wamphyri. As unimaginably long-lived creatures, to maintain the balance of nature they must breed very seldom. Reproducing asexually, each engenders his clone by secreting a single seed, which penetrates the new host's skin like a drop of acid and makes its way into the vital organs.

In his long-term seduction of Dragosani, Thibor rationalizes the Wamphyri life cycle and feeding behavior as no more repellent than the biological patterns of any other life-form. Both human beings and vampires are "parasites" as are "all living things" (318). Evil is nothing but "a state of mind", and human beings, after all, "devour the flesh of beasts and the blood of the grape"; all creatures "devour lesser lives" (169). Thibor maintains that "a vampire is no less natural a creature than the lamprey or the leech, or even the humble flea" (318). The vampire, he claims, is "kinder" than other animals, because "his host lives, becomes near immortal, and is not consumed in the normal manner of massive parasitic possession" (318). As *Homo sapiens* and Wamphyri developed together, the vampire, originally capable of living independently, grew irrevocably dependent upon humanity, which has "evolved into the perfect host" (318). The image of symbiotic cooperation that Thibor insinuates into Dragosani's mind is undercut by the allusion to animals such as leech and flea, considered repulsive by most people. Moreover, these creatures, as well as the "hagfish" (318) the vampire also uses as an analogy, possess no higher intelligence and, presumably, no emotions, only appetite and rudimentary survival instincts. Superficially, Thibor's argument resembles the ecological theme underlying such works as *The Vampire Tapestry;* the Wamphyri's rapacious destructiveness, however, culminating in the absorption and annihilation of the host's individuality, is a far cry from Weyland's comparatively benign predation.

Dragosani, after consolidating his position by beheading Thibor, completes his transmutation into a monster in human shape. Harry, Dragosani's structural counterpart in the novel, has also undergone a transformation, although psychic rather than physical. Through his experiences in the Mobius continuum (essentially a time-travel mechanism), meeting the dead from far-flung historical eras, he has "inherited a great sum of talents and now surely transcended Homo sapiens" (495). Now both Dragosani and Harry are "alien beings" (495), one predatory and the other altruistic, and each meets the fate suited to his character. The potentially immortal vampire, ironically, suffers death at Harry's hands, while the necroscope, although physically slain by Dragosani's gun, leaps free of his body to find immortality in the Mobius continuum. While Harry moves into the future, in search of the point where his "broken life-thread continued", exploring "the blue infinity of tomorrow", Dragosani is condemned to follow the "scarlet thread" that represents his "vampire-ridden past" (499). This cycle of futility effects a retrograde motion that inserts him into the body of Thibor at the moment when Dragosani's own blow strikes off the undead creature's head.

Later in the series we learn that the Wamphyri, rather than originating in our world, have infiltrated from an alternate dimension. This revelation connects Lumley's vampires with the Lovecraftian influences more clearly visible in Lumley's earlier work. Like Lovecraft's extradimensional invaders, the multimorphic aliens of the Necroscope series do not belong on Earth, but illegitimately seek to usurp the realm proper to humanity. *The Source* (1989) reveals that the Soviet ESP intelligence team has discovered an interdimensional portal in the Ural Mountains, a gateway into the world of the Wamphyri. The Cold War model continues to shape the plot, with Western and Soviet goals and methods contrasted in simple "good-evil" terms. The unscrupulous ruthlessness of the Russian antagonists is demonstrated by their willingness to tamper with the interdimensional gate. With the entry of British agent Jazz Simmons into the vampires' realm, the story undergoes a generic shift from horror to fantasy. From this point on, exploration of the alternate dimension, where human tribes struggle for survival under the threat of Wamphyri conquest, dominates the series. In their own world the Wamphyri rule a complex society, rather than functioning as mere parasites. The shaping of living flesh into genetically engineered slave creatures and even into structural components of their "aeries" takes the place of technology as human societies know it. The very walls of a Wamphyri aerie are formed of "the fused, polished bones and the hard, leathery hides of what were once men" (307). The Wamphyri play the role of a master race by using not only the inanimate world but living creatures, including human beings, in the mechanistic way human culture in the primary world often uses plants, animals, and the natural environment. In the vampire world, human beings fill the role of hunted animals and oppressed "lower" races. Like Lovecraft's nonhuman entities, the Wamphyri exert their dominance over humanity without regard for the rights of other sentient beings, but Lumley's vampires target victims with active malice rather than Lovecraftian cosmic indifference.

Once the story moves from Earth to the vampire realm, however, the Wamphyri are no longer portrayed as uniformly and simplistically evil. They begin to display individual personalities. One in particular, Lady Karen, retains some human traits. In *The Source* she bathes obsessively, as if trying "to scrub the taint out of herself", for there still exists "inside her a poor frightened girl" (309). Although a leader in her own right, not "vulnerable", Karen "for the moment perhaps still thought like a young woman", but the appearance of humanity is "only a shell" (313). Yet, as a female intelligence agent explains to Jazz, "the Wamphyri *are* human; it's the vampire in each one of them which makes him alien, and Karen's vampire had yet to gain total ascendancy" (313, Lumley's emphasis). Lady Karen sides with the human protagonists in a cataclysmic war against the vampire oppressors. In place of the parasitic or demonic-possession model presented in *Necroscope,* in *The Source* and the subsequent volumes we find a picture of human individuality in tension with the indwelling vampire, striving to maintain a balance. To complicate the picture, later in the series Harry Keogh himself admits a vampire into his inner self and unites with the entity. Furthermore, his son, Harry Junior, finds his way into the Wamphyri realm and also becomes tainted with vampirism, yet remains one of the "good" characters. Known as the Dweller, he rules a garden enclave, a haven for the human insurgents against Wamphyri rule.

In *Blood Brothers* (1992), when most of the Wamphyri have been killed or driven into the northern wasteland, one of Harry's twin sons by a Gypsy woman grows up as vampire, yet retains his individuality. Nathan, the twin who inherits Harry's necroscope gift, can sometimes forge a telepathic link with his vampiric brother, Nestor. In his brother he senses "a great rage of pain and frustration," a confusion "as if Nestor's mind was undecided about his identity" (320). The twins suffer estrangement because of their divergent destinies, but also because of rivalry over a Gypsy woman, Misha, whom Nathan marries. Although Nathan follows Harry Keogh in devotion to the cause of "good", the Gypsies, or Szgany, view both brothers with suspicion, on account of their father's vampiric infection. "Good" and "evil" are no longer defined by immutable boundaries, as in *Necroscope,* and characters infiltrated by the vampire seed can now resist the taint. For example, Turgo, carrying a "foetal vampire" engendered by the eldest of Wamphyri, vows never to "drink the blood of men" and instead feeds on animals (120). Just as "good" and "evil" lose their fixity, likewise distinctions between "our kind" and "Other" become blurred or reversed. In *Blood Brothers* one of Harry Junior's followers sees this Harry, the Dweller, as a creature of "alien origins...a being from an unknown world, commanding awesome weapons and powers" (7-8); the "unknown world", of course, is our own. These changes in the series since its inception in 1986 reflect the geopolitical shift, during the same period, from a stark opposition between capitalist democracies and Communist dictatorships to a constantly shifting web of alliances and rivalries.

A world ruled by vampires, with *Homo sapiens* a hunted and oppressed underclass, also forms the unifying theme of the anthology *Under the Fang* (1991), edited by Robert R. McCammon, in which Dr. Weyland returns. "Advocates", a collaboration between Suzy McKee Charnas and Chelsea Quinn Yarbro, appears to take place in an alternate-universe present, since Weyland retains the name he used in *The Vampire Tapestry* and therefore has not passed through the oblivion of the long sleep. Yarbro's character, Count Saint-Germain, assumes the task of defending Weyland against the charge of attacking other vampires. From Weyland's viewpoint, the undead, whom he had previously regarded as no more than a myth, are not true vampires, but merely an unusual variety of human. He informs Saint-Germain, "I am not of your kind, except in hunter's mimicry" (139). Since ordinary human beings have become difficult to hunt, he preys on vampires during their daylight sleep. Because their blood is "secondhand" and therefore "not very satisfying food", he must drink large quantities, plunging the victim into an irreversible coma (140). In this story Weyland reverts to the stark necessities of survival, with no need for even the cynical facade of humanity exhibited by his persona in the opening section of *The Vampire Tapestry*. Unable to conceal his scorn for the undead, he tells Saint-Germain, "I loathe the whole squabbling lot of you" (140). As for the human mobs who gather outside his prison claiming to worship him as a god for destroying the vampires who prey on them, and the vampires who revere him as the Antichrist, Weyland realistically expects no benefit from them. He knows that if he were delivered into their hands, he would probably "be chopped into relics" (142). Meanwhile, one of the vampire authorities, Inspector Samson, offers Weyland ostensible protection in exchange for the right to experiment on him. These two false escape routes parallel the dead-end possibilities he faces during his imprisonment in "The Land of Lost Content" in *The Vampire Tapestry.* "Advocates", however, offers no true escape; Weyland must stand trial at the mercy of vampires, since the human underclass has no power.

The world of "Advocates" frames Weyland as a cunning and dangerous beast, in contrast to the "civilized" vampires who put him on trial. Both Saint-Germain and Weyland see clearly that Weyland serves the vampire government as a useful test case. Saint-Germain expresses the necessity for vampires to "learn what it is to be civilized, to tolerate each other" (147). Their treatment of Weyland will determine whether they are "hunting animals or creatures with--souls" (147). Weyland perceives that this argument makes him into an object: "I am to be your lesson, then? Your example? Of the hunting animal you hope to transcend" (147). He angrily challenges the majority's determination "to build your damn civilization on my back" (147). Admitting the moral ambiguity of his position, Saint-Germain acknowledges, "Not that humanity offers any model much better than our own", but invokes the potential for "compassion" (147). Literally alienated from both undead and *Homo sapiens,* "thousands of years older than anything remotely akin" to him, Weyland scorns what he sees as Saint-Germain's weakness (147). The Count, in rebuttal, maintains that he progressed beyond Weyland's present behavior "more than four thousand years ago" (147). Acknowledging his kinship to humanity, Saint-Germain possesses the capacity for growth, while Weyland, enmeshed in the animal struggle for survival, does not change. In this world, with the human race relegated to the periphery--as "herds, or protected allies, or fugitives" (138)--and the undead in the center, vampires must build a culture and society to fill the vacuum left by the collapse of human civilization. With their numerous factions (such as Beaux, Cybertooths, and Fundamentalists) and political machinations, in effect the undead (like the victorious mutants at the conclusion of *I Am Legend*) have become the new humanity. Saint-Germain believes that vampires must "accept the bonds of blood" and thereby "accept the ties of life as well, and...revere it as no mortal human can" (155). To preserve their claim to humanity, they must not kill Weyland. Saint-Germain pleads with the court to exile the defendant to a reservation "where he can hunt or sleep, as he wishes" (155). (Since Weyland cannot live on animal blood, this solution, incidentally, implies that he will be allowed to feed on whatever human victims he can catch, a possibility that undercuts Saint-Germain's claim of reverence for life.) Assuming the dominant role formerly held by *Homo sapiens,* the ruling vampires, ironically, are prepared to treat Weyland as real-world human authorities would treat the last survivor of an endangered species of animal.

Kim Newman's *Bad Dreams* (1990), unlike his monumental historical novels *Anno-Dracula* (1992), *The Bloody Red Baron* (1995), and *Judgment of Tears* (1998), which feature supernatural vampires, portrays another nonhuman vampire who appears to be the last remnant of his species. Isolated by the death or disappearance of all other members of his race, "the Kind", the vampire, "Skinner", unlike Miriam in *The Hunger*, does not react to this isolation by turning to human beings for companionship. Skinner maintains a stance of superiority to and detachment from his prey. Although outwardly human in appearance, he is capable of radical physical transformation and healing from near-dismemberment. Virtually immortal, he renews his youth by feeding on the emotions of mortals, as well as, occasionally, their flesh and blood. In the past the human majority has struck back with "the traditional remedies", such as "hawthorne and rosewood stakes" and "silver-coated scythes", but only decapitation has proven successful, for the Kind "did not give up life easily" (42-43). Although they represent the truth behind humanity's superstitious fears, the Kind transcend the monsters of legend. A present-day victim recognizes the futility of "crucifix or wooden stake or pistol-load of silver bullets or flaming torch or hammer and sickle or bell, book and candle" and yearns instead for "Uzi sub-machine guns, or an anti-personnel rocket launcher" (247). The Kind are "as old as humanity itself", with a "secret history"; they have "withdrawn entirely from the affairs of men...to the shrinking white spaces on the map", aside from the brief period when Skinner ruled as their king (40). Since the downfall of his kingdom, he has lived in isolation among his human prey. His telepathic power creates the Dream, a mental landscape where the souls of victims he has devoured exist perpetually in a sort of undead condition. The heroine, Anne, recognizing Skinner as the "Monster" who, decades earlier, destroyed her father during the McCarthy hearings, wins the strength to survive and escape the Dream. She and her sister Judi, one of the drained victims, use the power of human cooperation and love to overcome the solitary, egoistic predator. Borrowing the life-force of all the other ghosts inside Skinner, Judi produces "a Hiroshima firestorm" (272) within him, reducing him to helplessness and disintegration.

The dark side of humanity, however, also figures prominently in *Bad Dreams*. The vampire's inhuman evil stands alongside the horrors of war, murder, torture, the McCarthy witch hunts, and the sadomasochistic club formed by Skinner to entrap potential victims (but enthusiastically embraced by his human dupes). At one point, near death at the hands of paid assassins unaware of his true nature, Skinner reflects, "If people habitually treated each other like this, who could blame the Kind for the way they treated the human race?" (55). Yet the subhuman imagery Newman applies to the Kind frames them as so remote from humanity that their evil surpasses any human transgressions. Unlike Weyland, metaphorically portrayed as an alluringly untamed carnivore or raptor, the Kind are described in repellant terms as reptiles or even lower life forms. When buried alive, Skinner frees himself by burrowing upward "through the loose rubble like a manta ray negotiating the complex cross-currents of the deep" (42). His lover Giselle feeds by "inflating her throat like a toad's to accommodate the gush of blood" (43). Skinner preys on a girl by "forcing his long tongue into her throat, latching suckerlike to her tonsils" (87). He has "venom glands" like a snake (264) and once appears with "hundreds of teeth...ruby-red and shark-sharp" (266). He tells Anne, "I'm just a thing of nature, like you...I'm no more the Devil than an alligator or a trap-door spider is" (265).

Anne, however, sees him, not as an innocent product of evolutionary forces, but as a Monster who is all facade without substance, who "could have been wearing a tissue paper death mask" (265). When she suggests, "There ought to be a protection order out on you. You don't want to wind up like the dodo or the passenger pigeon" (239), she expresses mockery, not sincere concern. Skinner's hint that he might transform her into his likeness provokes the retort, "You mean I could live forever, see the world, torture people and bite the heads off lizards? That's an awfully tempting offer" (239). The Monster's final transformation into "dry and crinkly" layers of skin, "[p]rogressively older, progressively less human-seeming, progressively deader", finally reduced to "rotting fragments" (276), validates Anne's struggle to maintain her individuality and Judi's choice of clean death over eternal undeath as part of Skinner's Dream.

The nephelim in Tim Powers' *The Stress of Her Regard* (1989) pass for human by shapeshifting rather than by "hunter's mimicry" like Weyland and Skinner or by infiltration and possession of human hosts as do Lumley's

Wamphyri and Wilson's space vampires. In contrast to the political model employed by Lumley, *The Stress of Her Regard*, set in the Romantic period, frames vampirism as an all-consuming and irresistibly seductive source of artistic inspiration. The nephelim's tactics of illusion and erotic enticement, as opposed to the invasion and conquest practiced by the Wamphyri, befit Powers' use of vampirism as a metaphor for art. Powers' work also partakes of the "paranoid style", however; his novel rewrites literary history by postulating that alien machinations underlie crucial events in the lives of the major Romantic poets. Keats' birth at the season of Halloween attracted the attention of one such creature, which killed his mother. Shelley has one of the nephelim for a half-sister. Byron has been stalked since the age of fifteen by Lord Grey de Ruthyn, the prototype of Lord Ruthven in John Polidori's "The Vampyre". Shelley and Byron owe their inspiration to the vampires, and their attempts to break the bond lead to disastrous consequences. After Shelley's death by drowning (a deliberate self-sacrifice to escape from his lamia), his heart is used in a ritual to drive the nephelim into dormancy "for the first time in eight hundred years" (465). The protagonist drawing together the multifarious, intertwined plot threads is Michael Crawford, who, the night before his wedding, places his future bride's ring on the hand of a statue of Venus. The statue, actually an ancient, silicon-based life-form, crushes his wife Julia to death on their wedding night. Julia's twin sister, Josephine, goes insane. Later, however, she becomes Crawford's ally against the nephelim, and they eventually marry.

In addition to the legend of the man who accidentally marries the goddess by placing his ring on a statue's hand, Powers' novel associates the vampire species with a plethora of mythical motifs. These creatures bear the name "nephelim" from Genesis 6:4 (there spelled "Nephilim"), in which the "sons of God" mate with ordinary women and beget giants. The Gorgons, the serpentine lamiae, the stones transformed into human shape to repopulate the earth after the Flood, the vampires of Greece and Eastern Europe, the Sphinx, Lot's wife crystallized into a pillar of salt, and the Graiae (the three witches who share a single eye among them) all originate in the secret lore of the nephelim. Like Williamson's witch-folk and Collins' Pretenders, Powers' vampiric aliens form the basis of a worldwide network of myths and are known to humanity only through the distorted memories of legend and superstition. Unlike many of the vampires discussed in the previous chapter, these apparently have no desire to reveal themselves to humanity. The artistic genius they bestow in exchange for blood and life-force is a snare in itself, an integral part of their predation. In this novel the Other functions as a metaphor for art consuming the artist and, oblivious to conventional moral standards, everyone around him. The creative drive becomes an addiction, analogous to the literal addiction to the nephelim's embrace suffered by the "neffers", former victims who gather to imbibe each other's blood in a futile quest for the ecstasy they once enjoyed. While ordinary victims get only strange, vivid dreams from this association, to those whom the vampires consider "family" they behave as Muses. Byron rebels at last because he loathes the thought that the vampire "was responsible for my--life's work, my writing, the thing that...made me *me*" (254, Powers' emphasis). He prides himself on writing *Don Juan* unaided by preternatural influence. Watching Josephine trying to wean herself from the compulsion to invite the draining of her blood, Crawford recalls from his own similar experience "how hard it was to do without that erosion of personality, once one had grown used to it" (408). Josephine speaks of the temptation "to stop being me", to become "just a walking--thing" (408). What may first appear as creative ecstasy reveals itself as the annihilation of the victim's human self. Standing above and apart from humanity, the nephelim, like the Wamphyri, provide another example of parallel evolution. In contrast to the carbon-based life represented by humanity and the rest of the known plant and animal kingdoms, these silicon-based entities are in effect living stones. They are "Lilith's people", "the *Siliconari*", "the first intelligent race the earth had", whose skeletons are composed of "the stuff that's the basis of glass and quartz and granite" (309). At some point in prehistory the nature of sunlight changed, so that prolonged exposure to its rays petrifies their bodies. A certain triad of stone pillars in Venice consists of the remains of the Graiae, "shackled by having certain restricting designs cut into their bodies" (181). Their "eye", their power of sight, actually signifies the power to know present and future events with absolute deterministic certainty, "down to decimal points even finer than God Himself ever bothered to figure to" (181). Their eye "forbids all randomness, all free will" (181). Conversely, when they are awake but blind, indeterminacy reigns in their vicinity, making the normally impossible possible (a circumstance the protagonists use to overcome the nephelim). This theory typifies the many instances where Powers draws upon twentieth-century quantum physics, genetic research, and evolutionary biology to rationalize the nature of his vampires. He also rationalizes their vulnerabilities to wood, iron, garlic, and mirrors in terms of modern physics.

The nephelim/lamiae, like the medieval incubi, can assume either sex and can plant their seed in a human female's womb. They can transmute themselves into many forms, a power that requires the drinking of human blood, because they need "the plan, the design, that's in the blood" in order to mimic human shape (183). A vampire in the semblance of Polidori tells Josephine, "Identity is not as rigidly quantized with us as it is with you. We're like the waves that agitate a body of water... Even the seeds we plant in people's blood aren't physical things, but a sort of maintained attention" (326). People drained to death by vampires arise from the grave, but no longer as truly themselves. Shelley explains, "Eggshells is all humans are to these things"

(265). In the grave, "the spores replace the organic stuff of their dead host with their stonier substance", as in the process of petrification that creates fossils (265). Whether any part of the victim's soul survives within the newly created vampire remains uncertain; however, the transformed corpse does have the ability to access the host's memories. Like Collins' Pretenders, the nephelim use the contents of the host's brain as a template. The creatures appear in a variety of shapes: phantoms mimicking people they have killed; a woman "pearly white and smooth", with "weirdly metallic eyes" (319); a "winged stone lion" with the face of Polidori (455); a "mad-faced, eyeless giant" (125); a thing on "elephantine legs" whose "torso seemed to be a huge bag at one moment and a boulder in the next", with a hide "bumpy like chain mail", yet recognizably feminine (76); a "knotted and lumpy" mass of cloud, shaped partly like a huge water serpent and partly like a "naked woman" (7); and even a rainbow. Their protean nature emphasizes their radical inhumanity. While their victims may labor under the delusion of being loved by the nephelim, their "love" is actually a devouring possessiveness. The novel frames entanglement with the nephelim as entirely negative.

Another *roman a clef* of the Romantic movement, *In Silence Sealed* (1988) by Kathryn Ptacek, also attributes major events in the lives of Byron, Keats, and Shelley to vampiric influence. The Greek sisters Athina and August are lamiae from classical mythology, inhuman creatures who drink the blood of children and creative geniuses, also feeding on the creativity of artists and poets along with their blood. They do not have the multimorphic powers of the nephelim, nor are they quite so ancient and alien; their bodies, apparently, resemble those of human females in many respects. Like their prototypes in Greek myth, Ptacek's lamiae are all female. Unlike the nephelim, they do not even offer the destructive inspiration so tempting to Powers' characters. Drawn to human artists, Ptacek's lamiae drain their essence without giving anything in return except short-lived sexual ecstasy. The vampires of *In Silence Sealed* do not appear to function as a metaphor for art; instead, they represent a mindless, destructive sensuality that vitiates creative genius by draining away its vital energies.

In a postmodernist blurring of boundaries between literature and history, Brian Aldiss' *Dracula Unbound* (1991) allows Dracula, Van Helsing, and Renfield to coexist in the same universe with Bram Stoker, Henry Irving, and Oscar Wilde. A time-traveling train shifts the action among Utah in 1999, London of the 1890s, and a distant, apocalyptic future ruled by a race of vampires, descendants of a humanoid species that lived in the age of dinosaurs. These creatures, would-be conquerors like Stoker's Dracula and Wells' Martians, reign over a world in which the human remnant will live enslaved as a food source for the master race. Aldiss' protagonists draw upon chaos theory, quantum mechanics, relativity, and the paradoxes of time travel in formulating their campaign against the aliens. They obtain a super-fusion bomb from the future to detonate it in the prehistoric past, thus preemptively exterminating the vampires but also causing mass extinctions, in what Ken Gelder calls "a 'fantasy of control' on a grand scale" (134). This novel frames vampirism as unequivocally negative. When one character proposes that "we should pity the poor vampires, doomed to such a miserable existence" and regard them as "really one more oppressed minority", Stoker declares that he simply views them as "a bad lot--a disease, in short" (181). Vampires inflict "[w]orse than death" upon their victims; they are "parasitical", analogous to "bedbugs, fleas, mosquitoes, ticks" (102-103). These creatures, "originally innocent suckers of fruit juice and plant juices", lost their Edenic innocence by evolving into consumers of blood (103). Because blood is "a dangerous beverage" and an "addiction like any other", these creatures--and by analogy, vampires--have "become enslaved by parasitism" (103). Thus an "aerial predator," a natural product of evolution, metamorphoses into a demonic "pestilence that walketh in darkness" (103). Like syphilis, the illness that afflicts Stoker, vampiric influence apparently has "the ability, in common with a disease of the brain, to erase engrams and deface memory" (159). A "pestilence" that can erode identity in this way holds a particular horror. Vampires, moreover, ensnare their victims "by activating one of the strongest instincts below the neocortical level, the great archetype of sex" (102). This sexual allure entails no mutual exchange between lover and beloved. Rather, the alien eroticism dehumanizes, operating through mindless biochemistry, like the scent of a flower. Thus the text shrouds its alien vampires in images of parasitism, disease, addiction, subhuman appetite, sexual corruption, and enemy invasion, as well as "total perversion" and "Christianity turned upside-down" (171). The Victorian plague, syphilis, invokes the contemporary parallel of AIDS. David A. Skal notes the similarities of both AIDS and drug addiction, in popular belief, to the stereotypical manifestations of vampirism: AIDS constitutes "a wasting malady involving blood", with "each victim creating more of his kind", while addiction involves "uncontrollable cravings and personality transformations" (*The Monster Show*, 349). It is not surprising that metaphors of addiction and venereal disease pervade both Aldiss' novel and Dan Simmons' "Dying in Bangkok", discussed below. As Nina Auerbach points out, Aldiss "more absolutely" than other authors "segregates vampires from mortals", for his aliens with "rudimentary brains and collective consciousness" are "merely, dangerously, mindless" creatures with no individuality and no neocortex" (176). As more "disease" than sentient beings, they inspire Stoker to write "the great vampire novel", which is also "the great syphilis novel" (Aldiss, 162). After helping to annihilate the aliens, he figuratively immortalizes them in a memoir disguised as fiction.

Another work that envisions a distant future ruled by vampires, Brian Stableford's "The Hunger and Ecstasy of Vampires" (1995), also features time travel and a cast of characters partly adopted from actual history. Oscar Wilde and H. G. Wells, among others, join Sherlock Holmes and Dr. Watson in listening to an experience recounted by a traveler, Copplestone, who uses a drug rather than a machine to propel his consciousness forward in time. He arrives in a future so far distant that the nineteenth century is recalled only in legends. The human species, having destroyed its own civilization, has been reduced to the status of domestic animals in a world under the domination of vampires. One female vampire justifies this ascendancy in evolutionary terms, maintaining that "the law of life" dictates that, "New species emerge, achieve dominance, and are superseded in their turn" (354). She claims, however, that her kind will never be superseded, because their species has become "master of its own evolution" (355). Originally they fed on mammalian blood and "lived invisibly on the margins of human society by virtue of their powers of mimicry" (355). In the distant future, they have outgrown the need to consume living blood and created a vampire utopia in which humanity has become superfluous. Copplestone's listeners, though fascinated by his tale, regard it as a vivid drug-induced hallucination--all but one, the narrator, whose vampiric nature is revealed at the story's conclusion. He steals the drug in order to flee from the present-day "sunless world of dismal madmen" into a "glorious world where violent and vapid mankind was naught but a myth and a memory" (390). Stableford's novella, in contrast to *Dracula Unbound*, privileges the vampire race over *Homo sapiens*.

Like the works of Powers and Ptacek, Dan Simmons' "Dying in Bangkok" (1993) also uses eroticism, addiction, and art as background for predation by superficially human alien vampires. Simmons' Mara and her daughter Tanha, however, do not share the antediluvian power and longevity of Powers' nephelim or Aldiss' vampires; Simmons' creatures are vulnerable to disease and appear to age at a human rate. These monsters use erotic artifice, onstage sex shows in Bangkok's roughest district, to drain nourishment from willing victims. Men pay exorbitant fees for the privilege of exposing themselves to audiences while Mara's grotesquely long, prehensile tongue with its razor-edged suckers drains the blood from their penises. The ecstasy of this experience overrides pain and fear. Spectacle and seduction become one and the same. The yellow-eyed *phanyaa mahn naga kio*--"demon-human incarnate" beings indwelt by the spirit of the serpentine *naga*--are alien in ethnicity as well as species (60). Through the eyes of the narrator, Dr. Merrick, who tells the double story of his first visit to Bangkok, on R and R from Vietnam in 1970, and his final return there to die in 1992, images of Otherness pervade the novella. By the time of his 1992 visit, Merrick knows the city and its language and customs. As a sophisticated traveler, he compares and contrasts Bangkok with his home, Los Angeles, both metropolises ironically known as "City of the Angels", both in the throes of mob violence (38). He refers to "androgynous Thailand", where it is hard to distinguish boys from girls in the red-light districts (43); analogously, the distinction between human and Other poses a seductive but dangerous mystery. The present-day Merrick, like his younger self, views the city in sexual terms, but now he is also fully cognizant of its deadliness, perceiving "the pollution and the stink of the river" as "an urgent scent like a subtle blend of exotic perfume, the Clorox tang of semen, and the coppery taste of blood" (40). The narrative intertwines images of erotic perversion with those of disease. In retrospect, Merrick comments about Thailand in 1970, "AIDS wasn't even dreamt of then" (49). In 1992, himself dying of the virus, he visualizes Bangkok as doomed to an apocalyptic AIDS plague, a place where "72 percent of the city's poorest prostitutes tested positive for HIV in 1989" and where by the year 2000, "far more than five million Thais will be infected and many more than one million will have died" (88).

As a young soldier in 1970, Merrick, like most of his comrades, knows only a few crude phrases of Vietnamese, enough to negotiate for sexual favors. He is even more ignorant of Thailand. His sexual naivete (he has yet to plumb the mysteries of oral sex and gives no thought to using condoms during his encounters with prostitutes) mirrors his insular attitude toward foreign cultures. Merrick's best friend Tres (pronounced "Tray") serves as a bridge to the alien world of the Orient. He speaks fluent Vietnamese and delves eagerly into the exotic culture of Bangkok. Reminiscent of the fatal drive to "dream outward" in Tiptree's story, the attraction of the Other lures Tres to his doom. Tres escorts Merrick on a pilgrimage to a heart of darkness, a descent into Hell symbolized by the movement from the familiar to the foreign, from ersatz American to the Orient. They progress from the enclave set aside for American soldiers and their "flophouse hotel" with a dozen prostitutes "hanging around the lobby" to more exotic attractions such as a "no-hands bar" (48), then from this relatively safe red-light district into the areas seldom seen by Westerners, by way of a hired boat along the "narrow one-way *klongs* [canals]" with their "blind turns" and "sagging bridges" hazardous with "rotting timbers" and a near-collision with "a high pier with its tall pilings rising ahead of us like a slammed portcullis" (52). Merrick gapes in wonder at a "blackened mass" of "tumbledown shacks and half-sunken *sampans*", despite his exposure to the horrors of war unable to comprehend that, "People *live* in those" (53, Simmons' emphasis). Images of strangeness, decay, and entrapment overshadow the journey. It culminates in the entry onto Mara's barge through a "corridor connecting the series of *sampans* and barges"; in blatantly Freudian symbolism, as he passes through the narrow opening, Merrick notes, "Strong smells came from it, and there was a muted sound rather like a large animal breathing somewhere down at the end of that tunnel" (54).

Through this metaphorical vagina he enters Mara's world, a realm of the demonic feminine as well as the alien. He witnesses her drawing blood from a customer and feeding it to her infant daughter, who licks her mouth with a long tongue that "slid like some pink worm across Mara's chin and lips", a gesture reminiscent of "baby birds demanding to be fed" (67). She regurgitates blood into the baby's mouth, similar to a vampire bat feeding its kindred. Years later, Merrick learns that "the roostmate's licking under the donor bat's wings and on her lips" stimulates the donor to regurgitate (68). A *Scientific American* drawing of two bats with "leathery wings entwined, slash-lipped mouths moving toward each other in the blood-vomit kiss" reminds him of the Thai vampires (68). The text continually draws analogies between these creatures and lower animals. The infant brings to mind "a tiny kangaroo baby, half-formed and almost embryonic, pulling itself through its mother's fur" (67). Tres compares the lesions on the victim's penis to the marks left by jellyfish stings. When Tres himself returns from a visit to Mara, he bleeds uncontrollably; Merrick is reminded of "a leech that breeds in the slow-moving waters of Vietnam that specializes in boring up the urethra of men wading in the water" (77). Later, as a doctor, he realizes that Mara secretes a natural anticoagulant like that produced by vampire bats and "European medical leeches" (79). When at last he makes his own visit to Mara and Tanha, he forces himself not to think of "the grasping mouth-guts of leeches and lampreys" (81). All these images hint that the Thai vampires are the products of natural evolutionary processes, but also that their human appearance is no more than a facade. Merrick finally concludes that although they are "monsters", they sometimes "grow careless" and "can be killed" (89). In contrast to Powers' nephelim, Mara and Tanha are framed as subhuman rather than superhuman monsters.

This novella, therefore, associates the Other with subhuman animal appetite (that rapaciousness, in turn, associated with the female principle) and with pollution and disease. Through the imagery of AIDS, moreover, these vampires, like those of Powers, are linked with addiction. Mara's feeding clearly has addictive properties, since Tres, although he returns to the hotel with dangerous bleeding from his genitalia, is determined to repeat the experience. Merrick's first exposure to Mara bestows on him the revelation "that someone might fuck even if it meant certain death", an insight that his older self associates with AIDS (73). Unable to stop his friend from embracing death, Merrick breaks his promise to accompany Tres back to Mara's barge and bears the guilt of this failure throughout his life. This guilt goads him to spend twenty-two years hunting for Mara and Tanha, until his HIV-positive status gives him the means to destroy them. This obsessive quest mirrors Tres' addictive response to the vampires. Only gradually does Merrick realize that he is driven by erotic love for his friend.

As a soldier in Vietnam, Merrick cannot admit his homosexuality even to himself. At that time, he rationalizes his love for Tres as "loyalty to a buddy, admiration, even the kind of masculine love that grunts are supposed to feel for one another in combat" (86-87). This unexpressed love and his self-blame for Tres' death haunt him, even driving away his present-day lover. Merrick has never come "out of the closet", his entire life shrouded in secrecy for the protection of his "public persona" as a successful doctor too busy for marriage (87). This concealment of his homosexuality, first from himself and then from the world, renders him metaphorically alienated. As noted earlier, contemporary fiction often draws parallels between vampirism and the gay subculture. Like the literal aliens of Simmons' novella, Merrick himself becomes an outsider. Both the vampire and the solitary, self-alienated homosexual stand on the fringe of human society. Merrick projects his guilt for Tres' death upon the "monsters". In the process of killing them through the ingestion of his own blood--"Death's blood" (89)--Merrick both punishes himself for allowing Tres to die and executes the "monsters" who perpetrated the murder. In death, he expiates his own crime and finally embraces "sleep and forgiveness" (89).

Numerous vampire novels from the late twentieth and early twenty-first centuries view the world through the monster's eyes. Those discussed in the previous chapter tend toward reconciliation, foregrounding the parallels between human and nonhuman to reveal that the "inhuman" need not equate to "evil". Others, however, like Anne Rice's Vampire Chronicles, tell their stories from the monster's point of view without portraying the inhuman as anything other than monstrous. Vampire characters in the latter type of fiction tend to embrace their monstrosity. Instead of regarding the vampire from outside as an enemy to be destroyed, as do the works of Lumley, Powers, and Simmons, these narratives present their vampires--although similarly rapacious and destructive--from inside, as protagonists with whom the reader is invited to identify. Those to be analyzed in this chapter all portray the alien vampire as an adolescent or young adult immersed in the ordeal of discovering his or her alien nature. These works frame vampirism as a metaphor for the adolescent identity crisis. Portraying the young protagonist as a vampire externalizes the typical teenager's sense of alienation from the adult world. In these novels, the teenager is literally an alien. The estrangement that often engenders fantasies of being a foundling unrelated to one's supposed parents finds expression in stories of children who discover this fantasy to be the truth of their lives. The unfolding of their vampire nature represents a rite of passage from childhood to adult self-determination, acted out in rebellion against the strictures of culture and law. From the adult viewpoint, the vampire image literalizes the not uncommon feeling, among parents of teenagers, that their offspring have transformed into alien monsters.

The boy Nothing in Poppy Z. Brite's *Lost Souls* (1992), a thoroughly decentered, postmodernist novel of literal and metaphorical alienation, discovers his anomalous past at the age of fifteen and takes to the road as a runaway. Brought up by adoptive parents under the name of Jason, Nothing is the offspring of a casual encounter between the vampire Zillah and a human girl, Jessy. Brite's vampires father children upon human females, who always die in childbirth. (Female vampires, who seem to be rare, also invariably die from the violent births of their infants.) An older vampire, Christian, who owns a bar in New Orleans, takes care of Jessy after her abandonment by Zillah, who is unaware of the girl's pregnancy. After Jessy's death, Christian leaves the baby on a doorstep in Maryland, with the ironic note, "His name is Nothing. Care for him and he will bring you luck" (11). As a teenager, Jason/Nothing takes up smoking and drinking, uses pot and other recreational drugs, dyes his hair black, skips school, consorts with "punkers", experiments erotically with friends of both sexes, "rips [his clothing] to rags before he'll wear it," and wants to get his ears pierced (28-29). In short, he indulges in all the behaviors most feared by parents of the nineties. His adoptive parents, caricatures of middle-aged incompetence, have nothing positive to offer: His mother meditates with "rose crystals" and anxiously assures him, "I don't want to keep you from fulfilling yourself. I certainly don't want to decrease your potential" (28), while his father rages impotently against the boy's numerous transgressions. His English teacher, equally stultifying, fails at her vocation; her "hypodermic needle of higher learning" drains "every drop of its primal magic" from *Lord of the Flies* (29). When Nothing, the only student who has read and appreciated the novel, tries to verbalize his excitement about the story, he receives a rebuke instead of encouragement. Alone in his room, staring at the symbolic stars painted on the ceiling, he imagines "the ghosts of all the decades of middle-class American children afraid of complacency and stagnation and comfortable death" urging him to escape (29). Having unearthed amid his parents' memorabilia the long-hidden note that names him "Nothing", he flees toward Missing Mile, the home of a musical duo he admires, "Lost Souls?"-- names that echo the theme of alienation.

Afflicted most of his life by feelings of isolation, Nothing regards the discovery of his foundling origin liberating. He views his foster parents as "strangers" who "had taken him in, changed his name, tried to make him into one of their kind" (72). Though he does not yet know of his inhuman ancestry, instinct tells him that he is of a different "kind" from his adopted family. He rejects their world as containing "not a thing that he could claim as his own" (70). Like many a "normal" adolescent, he wonders "whether there was a place for him outside the elaborate juju of his room...whether he could ever belong to anyone" (70). Even at the age of twelve he feels drawn to blood and fantasizes about biting. He connects these urges with the realization "that he was alone and that he might be alone for a very long time" (72). The name Nothing does not make him feel "worthless", but rather enables him "to think of himself as a blank slate upon which anything could be written" (73). He sets out to find himself in an almost literal sense, for he discovers not only his vampire nature but his biological father, Zillah. Nothing makes his first kill for blood just before he is picked up by the vampire trio of Zillah, Molochai, and Twig. Sharing intimacy through sex and blood-drinking with Zillah, Nothing finds a surrogate family, "the only place where he had ever felt truly accepted" (157). To preserve this new relationship, he participates in the murder of his friend Laine, whom the vampires have also picked up on the highway. Faced with the choice between refusing Laine's blood and the alternative, to "die, or be alone, and never drink from the bottle of life again" (160), he chooses the vampire life over human morality. His momentary qualms are overwhelmed by the revelation that the "taste of blood meant the end of aloneness" (160). He has no hesitation in believing that his three new companions are real vampires, for "otherwise there was no hope for him, because he had always known he could not live his whole life in the real world" (158). Realizing that he had committed himself "to a life of blood and murder" and could "never rejoin the daytime world", he readily accepts that fate to escape aloneness. Only later does he learn that Zillah is his father. Halfheartedly trying to convince himself that he ought to feel ashamed of father-son incest, Nothing concludes, "In a world of night, in a world of blood, what did such pallid rules matter?" (232). His quest and its fulfillment form a dark reversal of the fairy-tale motif of the peasant who discovers himself to be a prince in disguise or the mortal who learns that he has elven ancestry. The protagonist's choice of "a life of blood and murder" is, of course, not uncommon in recent vampire fiction; Brite's novel, however, is unusual in that the reader is invited, throughout, to continue empathizing and identifying with the newly initiated vampire. While contemporary fiction's best-known vampire protagonist, Rice's Lestat, embraces the "evil" role culturally assigned to him, Nothing--once he stifles his scruples about killing Laine--devotes little or no thought to questions of "good" and "evil". Vampirism is simply his nature.

The alienation that Nothing assuages through attachment to his vampire family is paralleled in other characters. Ghost, one half of Lost Souls?, is set apart from others by the psychic gifts inherited from his white-witch grandmother. Steve, his friend and partner, almost loses his belief in "magic" during his "eleventh summer...poised at the last reach of childhood", threatened by a potential future of "a bachelor's degree in advertising or some such deathsome thing" (49). Ghost's friendship enables Steve to make the transition from childhood to adolescence without losing the "magic", symbolized by the music whose allure also represents liberation for Nothing. Throughout the novel, the adult world, "obtuse and threatening" (64), coterminous with the cultural mainstream, represents repression, coercion, and spiritual suffocation. The realm of human adulthood is principally represented by Wallace, father of Jessy, who ran away from home in search of vampires and disappeared. For the fifteen years since, Wallace has hunted for the vampire who destroyed her. Having been touched by the "finger of God", obsessed with guilt over his incest with Jessy, he yearns to avenge her death and thereby regain "his memories of a child who danced and laughed, of a child who loved him, who was not a dark creature of sex and blood" (80). His alienation consists of self-deception. Steve's girlfriend, Ann, follows Steve and thereby becomes entangled with the vampires, seduced by Zillah as well as her own self-deception. Cut off from her human life, she is also rejected by Zillah, who uses her only as a weapon to punish Nothing. Pregnant with a vampire fetus, she dies from ingesting a potion prepared by Arkady, another character with the paranormal ability to recognize vampires. Ghost, the most perceptive of the characters, perceives that Ann has been "bewitched" by "the opium of Zillah's spit [i.e., the addictive quality of the vampire's bite] and the poison juices of whatever grew inside her" (309). Ghost appears to embody innocence, and he judges Nothing to be "not evil" but "lost, as surely lost as Ann's child" (309).

The older vampire, Christian, suffers his own kind of alienation. His efforts to control the impulsive violence of the young vampires parallel the equally ineffectual authority of Nothing's foster parents. At one point Molochai, Zillah, and Twig "punish" Christian by forcing him to drink a large quantity of liquor that makes him violently nauseated. His impotent pleas to be spared the ordeal have no effect on Zillah and the others. He is helpless against them because losing their companionship would mean losing Nothing as well. He cannot face "the constant specter of loneliness", reduced to finding "moments of love" in the caresses he shares with his victims before killing them (335). His vain attempts to impose moderation upon the young vampires make him resemble a stuffily conservative father figure, but a permissive, indecisive one as well. He recognizes the futility of trying to "buy their love", for he can never be like them, "young and strong and wild", regarding blood as "just another path to drunken gratification"; to him, "the blood is life itself" (341). In the context of the novel, Christian's weakness seems to stem from his ethical and compassionate impulses, traits that, in the eyes of Molochai, Zillah, and Twig, make him less than a true vampire. He takes pity on Jessy and nurses her through her pregnancy, whereas Zillah never even stops to consider the possibility of conception. When Christian kills, he regrets taking a life even as he feels "a little less alone than he had been before" (68). He rationalizes that he shows kindness to his teenage victims by allowing them to believe they will rise as undead, even though in fact he and they belong to "separate races, races that were close enough to mate but still as far away from each other as dusk and dawn" (68). The other vampires, of a younger generation, physically tougher but without Christian's retractile fangs (they must file their teeth or use razors to draw blood), indulge in no such equivocations; they feel no need to excuse their predation. Christian, despite his pity for human victims, puts his own species first by trying to protect Zillah and the others against Wallace. Having seen no others of his own kind in far too long, he wishes for "the power that the legends ascribed to him", the power to make his victims "rise again and run with him" (90). He dislikes cutting short "the fragile span of their forty or fifty or eighty years"; unnecessary killing makes him "feel vicious and cruel" (100). Whenever possible, he prefers to hide or flee from discovery rather than fight back. For a vampire in this fictional universe, however, such restraint is not an advantage. Christian dies along with Zillah, leaving Nothing to wander with Molochai and Twig. Nothing leaves a message of love for Ghost, who summarizes the existential morality of the novel: "Maybe they were evil... My grandmother told me you shouldn't try to define evil, that the minute you think you've got it all pinned down, a kind of evil you never even thought of will sneak up behind you...I don't think anyone knows what evil is. I don't think anyone has the right to say" (354).

Sins of the Blood (1994), by Kristine Kathryn Rusch, centers upon another young adult vampire brought up by human adoptive parents, but Rusch's narrative does not repudiate conventional morality as decisively as Brite's does. Rusch's nascent vampire, Ben, has an older sister, Cammie, whose struggle to resist the vampire taint balances her brother's immersion in that way of life. The novel takes place in an alternate present where the truth of vampirism has been publicly known since the turn of the century. Cammie works for the Westrina Center, specializing in vampire investigation and eradication in one of several states in which destroying vampires is legal and considered admirable. Like Nothing, Cammie and Ben are cut off from the truth of their own past, their early childhood memories buried under layers of trauma. Cammie gradually unearths the memory of driving a stake into the heart of her vampire father to save her younger brother's life. She was trained as a vampire-hunter by the Westrina Center, while Ben was placed for adoption in a distant city. The narrative frames vampirism partly as a disease and partly as an addiction. For example, vampire victims not killed outright often become "codependents who helped the vampire survive by covering for it during the day and feeding it at night" (36). Since these "codependents" are often the vampire's own children, motifs of child abuse and incest also overshadow the novel. Besides its infectious phase, this kind of vampirism also takes a hereditary form, for a male vampire can father children for a short time after his transformation. Ben, as a hereditary vampire, has potential powers that the others envy. Now a recent college graduate, he discovers his bloodlust in a sexual encounter with his lover, Candyce. Soon thereafter, a new friend, Steve, introduces him to the vampire subculture. Like many young people on the verge of adulthood, Ben suffers from the sense that "his body felt as if it belonged to someone else" (22). Though vampire puberty begins late and lasts longer than the human developmental counterpart, its onset is also linked to the awakening of sexual desire. Among the vampires, Ben finds the cure for his self-alienation and, in the process, like Nothing, renounces human moral standards to fit into his new clan.

He begins with a stereotypical image of vampires as "derelicts with a taste for blood" (58) and "weak people who had been seduced by other weak people" (59). Mikos, his mentor, replaces his concept of vampires as diseased addicts with a vision of them as a superior race, "the chosen" (60). According to Mikos' social-Darwinian perspective, the "weak" vampires die off quickly, leaving the strong and intelligent, such as himself. Ben, though "aberrant" for a human, is "surprisingly normal" for a vampire "who has been trying to live with the very thing it eats" (60). The vampiric attitude toward their human prey is epitomized by the "cow bars", where people addicted to the "exquisite sexual high" (61) provided by the vampire's bite offer themselves as willing victims. Such individuals, whether men or women, are referred to as "cows", a term that depersonalizes by rendering them grammatically asexual as well as subhuman. They are "dessert" (59) or "dinner...nothing compared to us" (102), rather than persons. The female vampire Van, less overtly violent than Mikos, takes an equally pragmatic view of human beings, who "are not stupid" but "different"; vampires are "parasites that feed off them, and we are better off if they live" (80). She is no fonder of humanity than Mikos, only more cautious. Quickly bored with feeding and sexual indulgence, Ben awakens to the allure of the power promised him as a member of "the real race, not those...who had been turned [transformed]" (120). Having killed a man without remorse, Ben adopts Mikos' depersonalizing attitude toward humanity. He looks back upon the "life his parents had taught him, the career track he had been on, all those petty concerns about legalities and good grades and other people...as if that life had belonged to someone else" (118). His awakening to his vampire nature constitutes both a rebellion against parental and societal authority and the reinvention of himself as an alien, superior being. Having killed at Mikos' bidding, he declares himself "no longer...a good American boy" (119). Toward his girlfriend Candyce he becomes alternately brutal and manipulative. To him she becomes another "cow", for whom he cares only in the context of her role as a vessel for his unborn child, the potential future of the vampire race. The "hereditary child of a hereditary" holds the promise of extraordinary power (210). Mikos, however, allows Van to kill Candyce, purely to teach Ben a lesson--that he has allowed Candyce to matter "more...than a cow should" (202)--thus underscoring the low value the vampires place on human life. Ben suffers passing regret for Candyce's death and for the loss of the love they shared before his vampirism awakened, but he soon turns his attention to the search for a new woman upon whom to father a child.

Cammie's reaction to her latent vampiric tendencies contrasts with Ben's. At first, when her suppressed memories of childhood resurface, she takes refuge in denial: "There's no proof that vampirism is inherited" (268). Her training as a vampire-killer has imbued her with loathing for vampires, so that if she sees herself as one, she will be required to hate and destroy herself. She displays contempt for Dr. Brooker, an expert she meets in Oregon, which does not allow the eradication of vampires. Cammie regards Brooker as one of those "Western hicks" with "no concept of true vampirism" (269). Brooker, in turn, disapproves of institutions like the Westrina Center that "treat vampires like criminals instead of like people with an awful disease" (269). According to Brooker, vampires should be treated not with "simple counseling", proven ineffective in the 1960s, but also by "taking into consideration the physical changes the vampire goes through" (269). Cammie dismisses him as soft on vampires and clings to her belief in eradication as the only solution. The argument parallels real-world controversy over methods of combatting illegal drug traffic. Later, when Cammie finds Ben, she awakens to the bloodlust within her and barely stops herself from draining a man to death. When Ben reassures her that she will soon come to enjoy feeding, she reflects, "That was what she was afraid of... Someday she would think it all right to take a drugged man's life because he offered his blood to her" (363). Ben tries to seduce her with the promise of power, shifting the argument from the realm of morality to that of self-preservation and gratification: "They're afraid of us. That's why they teach you it's wrong... Imagine feeling like this for the rest of your life" (358). Cammie, however, does not feel "powerful" as a result of her indulgence in blood, but rather "outta control" (358). Ben is guided by his libido, she by her superego. In the end she recognizes the ineluctable alienation that renders her and her brother "forever doomed to be separate and different" (382), a realization encapsulated in their final dialogue before she executes him: He says, "I never thought you would have a conscience, Cam," and she replies, "I never thought you wouldn't" (381). Despite her love for Ben and even her long-dead father, she acts on the truth that "there was nothing in the world she hated more than vampires" (386). In the final scene she flees alone to the nearest rehabilitation center, determined to fight the craving and preserve her humanity. The disease/addiction model prevails over the "superior race" model.

Rusch's short story "Victims" (1995) also problematizes the "superior" status of vampires within the context of an alternate universe where creatures formerly believed imaginary have won public recognition. With a more sympathetic treatment of nonhuman characters than in *Sins of the Blood,* this story draws parallels between its female vampire, victimized despite her preternatural powers, and socially stigmatized women such as prostitutes. Even with vampires "out of the closet" and with public knowledge that most vampires "had long ago given up killing human prey--choosing instead to use a handful of willing people to provide blood," the "popular imagination" remains obsessed by "the sensual effect of the predator-victim relationship" (168). The narrator, Catton, in search of political ammunition against former California Governor Nichols, contacts Veronique de la Mer, the vampire owner of an escort service. Catton aims "to smear the former governor by linking him to a vampire as her cow", a strategy that he expects to "work as effectively as gay bashing" (169). Veronique refuses to cooperate with this strategy, instead claiming that Nichols raped her over twenty years earlier. At the time, the police dismissed her complaint because of her occupation. Now she expects still less sympathy, as a known member of "a completely different race" (169). Identified with prostitutes and ethnic minorities, Veronique cannot effectively demand justice. To make matters worse, human beings such as Catton cling to inaccurate legends and expect a vampire to change into a bat and rip out her attacker's throat. The popular perception of vampires as "the all-evil, all-powerful beings the movies have made them out to be" makes a female vampire's rape by a human male seem far-fetched (177). Veronique's nonhuman nature, however, does not make her invincible, but rather exacerbates her vulnerability. When Catton tells her that "Middle America" would not care about her rape, Veronique agrees, "Middle America would simply figure that a woman like me deserved it" (170). Determined to claim her self-respect, Veronique refuses "to be linked to that slime [Nichols] romantically or parasitically", but will cooperate only in exposing him as "a man capable of extreme violence" (170). Rusch's text identifies the vampire with the marginalized, silenced victims of entrenched patriarchal privilege. Veronique, her consciousness raised, claims her rights as a citizen by breaking the silence. One of Catton's associates articulates the principle that "victims are victims when they remain quiet" and "gain power when they speak out" (179). By choosing to play the victim's role, paradoxically, Veronique wins the political influence that her nonhuman "superiority" cannot bestow.

Scott Ciencin in *The Vampire Odyssey* (1992) and Pat Graverson in *Sweet Blood* (1992) present less ambiguous images of vampires as a master race. Both of these novels, though less complex than Brite's and Rusch's, work with plot motifs similar to those found in *Lost Souls* and *Sins of the Blood*. Ciencin's vampire child, Danielle, is found abandoned in a dumpster and adopted by Samantha Walthers, a private detective. As a teenager Danielle, like Nothing and Ben, finds her way into the vampire subculture, acting out through violence and promiscuity her rebellion against her foster mother's standards. In her adolescent investigation of the adult secrets hidden from children, she, like Nothing, discovers her difference from her supposed parent and her kinship with a superior species. Her new companions initiate her into thrilling powers such as flight and reveal the ancient mythology of their kind, "the bastard children of the Dark Angel" (163). Their revelations play up to her youthful sense of alienation and isolation, as well as the grandiose dreams typical of adolescence. She finds that she is not alone in her abandonment, that all female vampires are "left to die" in infancy, with their "true mothers killed because they bore a lowly female" (163). They are all "shunned by others of [their] kind" but, providing the home and family they each crave, they "have survived by finding one another, by teaching each other and ourselves that we have become what we were born to become. Immortal" (163-164). Danielle's residual love for her foster mother, however, struggles against the temptation to plunge completely into the vampire world. Samantha fights for her daughter and persists in reaching out to Danielle despite the girl's rejection. Finally Danielle, realizing that the vampires have lied to her, chooses Samantha over them. In contrast to *Lost Souls,* Ciencin's novel culminates in intergenerational reconciliation, though Danielle remains a vampire and, in two sequels, must deal with her ambiguous position between the vampire and human realms.

Graverson's seventeen-year-old vampire, Adragon, shares a different dynamic with his mother, Elsbeth, herself a vampire. The two of them have known each other through many lifetimes, reincarnated as siblings, parent and child, and lovers. Elsbeth has concealed Adragon's true nature from him only to wait for the proper moment, and she resents the attempt of a young female vampire, Del, to seduce him. Adragon wholeheartedly embraces violence, sexual excess, and a polymorphous-perverse incestuous relationship with Elsbeth. This novel's central conflict does not focus on human values as opposed to alien ones or the adolescent quest for self-knowledge in defiance of parental authority, but principally upon the mother's rivalry with the son's lover. Unlike Danielle, Adragon chooses his new companion, Del, over his mother, and his only significant rebellion consists of resolving his Oedipal conflict by rejecting his mother's erotic allure in favor of a younger woman's.

Although Graverson's novel takes place almost entirely within the vampire subculture, Adragon does at first believe himself to be human. Melanie Tem's *Desmodus* (1995) portrays a vampire community entirely detached from human society, a realm intersecting ours only where absolutely unavoidable. Like the self-absorbed supernatural vampires of the 1980s as characterized by Auerbach, they "live and love in enclaves of their own" (Auerbach, 186). Tem's novel completely reverses the alien-human polarity; to her protagonist Joel, his clan members are "people" and *Homo sapiens* the dangerous outsiders. (The text does not explain why these creatures adopt human-derived names and, apparently, speak no language except English.) Unlike most fictional vampires, Joel's species leads a gregarious communal life, tightly knit to the point of claustrophobia. Essentially intelligent, humanoid bats, they can pass unnoticed within human settlements only by covering themselves in voluminous clothing and taping down their ears. Besides their wings and ears, their other nonhuman features include fangs and long, curved nails, as well as less visible details such as echolocation, nocturnal activity, the anticoagulant in their saliva, and the ability to detect heat waves. Vampire bat characteristics foreground their biological distance from humanity, but unlike similar details in Simmons' "Dying in Bangkok", here these traits are not demonized or designed to arouse revulsion. Joel, as first-person narrator, regards behaviors such as feeding blood to infants by mouth-to-mouth exchange as ordinary facts of everyday life. For example, Joel remarks that a rumor spreads through the community "passed from one to another like partially digested food" (1). Their babies, like infant bats, stay together in a communal nursery, where mothers visit to feed them, each locating her own child by calling to him or her. Joel finds the nursery, "those large, snug rooms, fur-lined with the little writhing bodies of all those eternally ravenous babies," unsettling, but from masculine nervousness, not ordinary squeamishness (44).

Numerous other physiological peculiarities distinguish the Desmodus clan from *Homo sapiens,* notably their seasonal cycle of migration and hibernation. While the females, after an orgy of feeding and mating, withdraw into hibernation, the males migrate south each winter. To keep the clan together and safe, the vampires have adapted human technology; the men drive huge temperature-controlled trucks that shelter the dormant women. Females store semen from mating until the optimum time for ovulation, a process under conscious control to ensure that babies are born in the spring. Besides conserving energy, hibernation bestows upon women a "life-changing or -

centering, hallucinogenic" experience, "connected directly to the divine" (86). While Joel expresses some skepticism about these spiritual claims, he has no doubt that "because of our different metabolic patterns between winter in the south and summer up north, migration had turned out to be not nearly so effective an evolutionary adaptation as hibernation"; therefore, females live much longer than males and display "greater stamina, discipline, creativity, productivity, and all-around class" (103). Males are assumed to be, by comparison, irresponsible and dull-witted. Joel accepts as axiomatic that his life "and that of every other male, was congenitally incomplete" (87). As far beyond ordinary women as women are beyond men, the near-mythical Old Women remain permanently dormant, shrouded in a transcendent altered state of consciousness. Joel accidently stumbles upon an Old Woman inside one of the trucks. Her "distorted" body has, like younger members of their species, "four limbs and tail with scoop, but all the appendages were distended beyond recognition" (139). She emits a peculiar vibration "like a cosmic explosion", and he perceives her as an "inversion of radiant heat and consciousness like...a collapsed star" (138). The vampires' heavily female-dominant social structure emphasizes, for the human reader in our culture, their unlikeness to ourselves.

In their ecological relationship to human beings and other mammals, Tem's vampires take pride in "the demonstrable fact that we were able to sustain ourselves without harming any other living creature" (151). Joel admits to "feeling more than a little self-righteous" about this "metabolic peculiarity" that renders vampires "a definite minority among the world's species" (151). His mother says with displeasure, upon finding a shriveled, bloodless rabbit, "We don't take more than we need. Such lack of self-control. Such sadism" (94). They regard human beings, in contrast to themselves, as potentially dangerous creatures who might at any time unite into "a vigilante posse to exterminate us" (113). Rumor hints that some branches of their species "even lived in towns, among townspeople, in a kind of symbiosis that horrified" Joel (31). He knows that in the distant past his own family had closer contact with their human neighbors, "an ugly and hazardous period all around" (12). An "undercurrent of anxiety" circulates through the community whenever any of them must venture into town (11). Joel's viewpoint grants us a skewed vision of humanity, with "the same fearful bilateral symmetry, the same imploded and furious energy, the same hot blood" as his own kind, and yet different (16). Like numerous other vampire-as-alien novels, this text foregrounds the truth that we are all animals, but in *Desmodus,* the vampires are the standard against which other species are measured.

Joel's people remark upon the oddities of humankind just as human beings exchange speculation about people of other races. The males leer over the presumed hypersexuality of human females, who are "into fucking a lot more than our girls are... They don't have, like, seasons, you know. They can get it on anytime" (157), in an amusing reversal of the standard fictional convention of vampiric sexual insatiability. Oddly, young Rory, Joel's nephew, adopts human prejudices against blacks, homosexuals, and other minorities, having "little use for anybody who wasn't 'like me'," human beings and other breeds of vampires alike, and regards himself "as a lonely righteous being in a corrupt and alien world" (81). It is particularly strange, therefore, that the only individualized human character in the novel, Ernie, brought home by Rory as a sort of pet, is black. Rory sets aside his racism and homophobia to engage in sexual dalliance with Ernie, of whom he says, "But he ain't my friend. He's my slave. My *looove slave*" (193, Tem's emphasis). Joel perceives "a strong aura of sinister obscenity" in their sexual congress (192). When Joel questions Ernie about his reasons for staying with the clan, Ernie says he is estranged from his family and has nowhere to go; he represents the only instance in this novel of a human adolescent drawn to vampirism out of alienation from his own background. Rory alternates between dismissing Ernie as a "human whore" (259) and claiming to love him. A pair of misfits in their own families, they form a tenuous union. As for Joel, he tolerates Ernie but has no respect for him, since the human boy is "a stranger" and "an alien" (245).

Joel, in turn, becomes estranged from his clan when he assumes the gender-bending role of caretaker for the out-of-season infant born to one of his young female relatives, Meredith. Possessed by an unexpected love for the baby, whom he names Eli, Joel flees with the newborn when he discovers a secret that females hide from males: Women feed upon the brain fluids of infant boys, a habit that probably accounts for the stereotypical mental backwardness of men. Rory, eager to feed upon the baby, too, makes himself into an outlaw by pursuing Joel and Eli. Ernie, in turn, follows Rory. Joel conceals himself and the infant in a cave, reminiscent of the "dark underground chambers" in which their race evolved (274). Their mythology teaches that their "emergence into the upper world was...still incomplete, still incipient and even inchoate" (274). Through his vain attempt to save Eli's life, Joel achieves his personal vision quest, an endeavor beyond the scope of the average male. In the caverns he finds the waking counterpart of a recurring dream he has first invented to amuse his mother, then has actually begun to dream. After Eli's death he etches his own name on a cavern wall, written with his claws and stained with his blood, in fulfillment of the dream. As an epitaph to the baby, he adds, "BECAUSE OF HIS PASSING" (351). Whether he will return to the clan after this shamanistic ordeal (or whether, for that matter, Rory and Ernie will remain the rest of their lives in the cave, absorbed in mutual sensuality) remains unsaid. Having repudiated his culturally dictated masculine role, Joel has symbolically emerged farther into the "upper world" than thought possible for a male. His rebellion does not lead him to seek humanity, as the rebellion of Nothing and Ben drives them to seek vampirism.

Human influence does play a part in catalyzing Joel's quest, however, for the "alien" Ernie awakens him to the fact that Eli's mother is feeding on the infant's brain fluids. Otherwise, the realm of *Homo sapiens* is not only peripheral but irrelevant to the central concerns of Joel's life.

All the works discussed in this chapter foreground alienation rather than connection. Of those whose plots are constructed around vampire-human conflict, either a vampire or human protagonist may function as viewpoint character. When the principal perspective is human, as in Lumley, Powers, and Simmons, vampires are framed as enemies to be feared and destroyed. In novels narrated principally from the vampire perspective, as with Brite, Rusch, and Graverson (and, to some extent, Ciencin), human beings are framed as victims and food. "Advocates" foregrounds conflict among different vampire factions, relegating *Homo sapiens* to the fringe, with the "undead" taking over the role formerly played by human culture. Tem's *Desmodus* inverts and deconstructs the tropes of vampire-as-alien fiction, placing a fully developed vampire subculture at the center of the narrative and making humanity irrelevant.

Conclusion

For Love of Wonder

We recall that in *The Vampire Tapestry* Weyland articulates Floria's fascination with him and, by extension, speaks for all who recognize the allure of the alien among us: "As to the unicorn, out of your own legends--'Unicorn, come lay your head in my lap while the hunters close in. You are a wonder, and for love of wonder I will tame you'" (161). Fictional treatments that aspire to "tame" the "wonder"--the *monstrum*-- approach the taming in a variety of ways. The project of domesticating the monstrous, however, carries a weight of ambivalence; often the monstrous, in addition or instead, transforms the human. As Marina Warner says of our culture's recent "cascade of deliberate revisions" of the traditional "Beauty and the Beast" fable, "Beauty stands in need of the Beast, rather than vice versa, and the Beast's beastliness is good, even adorable... The Beast as a beast has become the object of desire" (307-309).

The earliest novels and stories scientifically rationalize the alien vampire as a part of nature, a product of evolution, yet employ the language of superstition, identifying their vampires with the ogres of folklore. These aliens appear as invaders and predators, with whom no rapport is possible. Human protagonists struggle either to escape from the monster or to "tame" it through conquest or outright destruction. Later the alien vampire is more likely to wear a human shape, and human characters may see themselves mirrored in the face of the monster. The alien may be portrayed as a foreign or extraterrestrial invader, a species parallel to and inimical to our own, or the next phase in human evolution. Communication between "our kind" and the Other becomes possible, even in works which ultimately frame the vampire as hostile or evil. The "evil" vampire survives to the present as one thread in the fictional web, but recent works allow glimpses into the alien's mind even while consigning the monster to damnation. Contemporary fiction presents the alien vampire as a multivalent figure, which may symbolize the threatening racial or sexual Other, the attractive Other, the persecuted ethnic minority, the artist (or, more often, the artist's inspiration), the rebellious adolescent, the bearer of plague, the endangered species--in short, the outsider in any of his, her, or its many guises. The vampire as literal alien serves as a vehicle for the exploration--and the containment--of metaphorical alienness. Writers of juvenile fiction, even more frequently than authors writing for adults, tend to emphasize the likenesses rather than the differences between vampire and human. Both adult and juvenile fiction may undercut the vampire's threat by portraying him or her as a persecuted outcast, often contrasted with a more threatening specimen of ordinary humanity. Other texts domesticate the vampire by stressing the monster's weaknesses, embodied in his or her dependence on human donors. This dependence becomes especially clear in romances, where the sexual bond between human and vampire lovers frames them as equals rather than predator and prey.

These various modes of "domestication" highlight the dominance of the sympathetic vampire in contemporary fiction. Although the traditional undead can also be found among the ranks of "good" vampires, the vampire as alien fits especially well into the neutral or admirable category. A character who owes his blood-thirst and other feral attributes to natural evolution cannot be blamed for what nature has made him. In keeping with the frequent metaphorical association between vampirism and homosexuality, we may draw an analogy with the hypothetical "gay gene". Though some people may still regard the bearer of a genetic tendency toward either homosexuality or blood-drinking as dangerous, he or she can no longer be demonized. In terms of repulsion and attraction, fictional vampires may be seen as occupying points on a continuum defined by three classifications--completely horrifying, completely attractive and benign, and simultaneously alluring and horrifying. For example, the Horla represents the first category, Petrey's Varkela the second, and Shambleau the third. Lumley's Wamphyri, except for a few individuals among them, remain near the first pole, while Lichtenberg's luren closely approach the second. Over the course of *The Vampire Tapestry*, Weyland progresses from the "horrifying" to the "attractive" end of the spectrum, without ever becoming as nearly "domesticated" as Petrey and Lichtenberg's aliens.

Since these texts (except for anomalies such as *Desmodus*, which attempts to present a completely alien perspective) necessarily incorporate the human viewpoint, whether a vampire is classified as morally "good" depends upon the character's attitude and behavior toward humanity. "Good vampire" fiction falls into two basic categories: (1) Vampirism as such is intrinsically evil or involves an inexorable pull toward evil; (2) vampirism is a morally neutral condition, and the subject's behavior can be virtuous or wicked on the same terms as other people's (allowing for the complication of the need to consume blood). Alien vampires, although not supernatural agents of the devil, can be framed as intrinsically "evil" if they are violent by nature and their nutritive requirements compel them to harm or kill human victims. In this kind of fictional universe, the only "good" vampire is the one who seeks a "cure" for his condition, like Joshua in *Fevre Dream* or the heroes of some romances. In such cases, the vampire who insists upon his or her superiority over the human race is, by definition, evil, framed as an exploiter and tyrant, even a rapist or murderer. The "good" vampire, in effect, is the one who denies his own nature and tries to "pass". He or she views even immortality as negative and embraces what the "evil" vampire would view as human "weakness". "If vampirism is a wasting disease like AIDS," as Auerbach remarks, "its cure is a blessing, but if it contains immortality, secret strength, and forbidden identities, its domestication is a death" (192). In fiction that defines the alien vampire's condition as morally neutral, the character who applies ethical standards to his relations with humanity, who avoids harming human beings--or, at least, avoids harming the "innocent"--qualifies as "good". This kind of vampire need not reject his alien traits and powers in order to live a moral life. He does not need to be "cured" of what he is (as Floria fears doing to Weyland), nor must he embrace the domestication-as-death postulated by Auerbach.

Turning from literature to film, we find this dichotomy illustrated by two television series, both of which feature traditional supernatural vampires but nevertheless cast light upon the "vampire as alien" category. The "cure" motif is central to *Forever Knight*. Nick Knight's quest to become "mortal" again dominates his existence. While seeking the elusive cure, he strives to atone for his past sins. His loathing for his vampire nature defines him as "good", and his commitment to the quest is symbolized by his habit of consuming refrigerated bovine blood instead of human blood. Naomi Janzen, supervising producer, remarks in an interview that "Nick has discovered...that mortals are actually something rather exalted, and vampires and evil are on a lower plane" (*Fangoria Vampires,* 167). Not coincidentally, *Forever Knight* emphasizes its vampires' formerly human status, with the vampire-human borderline presented as fluid and permeable (Nick enjoys a short-lived reversion to the human norm, his vampire lover Janette attains mortality, and in one episode a character manifests multiple personalities, only one of which has vampiric traits).

Kindred: The Embraced (derived from the role-playing game "Vampire: The Masquerade"), on the other hand, stresses the nonhuman nature of its vampires. They express no desire to revert to their original human condition, and they form their own subculture, complete with "clans", as if they were an alien species or at least a separate race. Mark Rein-Hagen, creator of "Vampire: The Masquerade", has one of his characters remark in *Book of the Kindred,* "Though our external appearance remains much like that of the living, there are those among us who insist that the Change transforms its subject into another species" (49). As portrayed in the television series, they do not classify their condition as inherently evil, nor do they pine for their lost humanity, but rather strive to live ethically as vampires.

At the end of the twentieth century, *Buffy the Vampire Slayer,* despite a theory of vampirism that defines the undead as corpses animated by demons, emphasizes the humanity rather than the alienness of its vampires. In the universe of *Buffy* and its spinoff *Angel,* vampires can eat and drink normal food and beverages, show the effects of caffeine and alcohol, and engage in sexual intercourse (but not, short of a miracle, conceive or bear children). These vampires are relatively weak compared to most in fiction and film, possessing few of the conventional powers such as shapechanging and hypnosis. (Dracula, who appears in only one episode, presents an anomalous exception to this pattern.) Moreover, Angel, like Nick Knight, spends one day as an ordinary mortal, then reverts to the vampire condition. His possession of a soul and the later restoration of Spike's also foreground these vampires' connection to their lost humanity.

All these series define their nonhuman characters in traditional supernatural terms. There are few instances of humanoid alien vampires in recent movies and television. Strieber's *The Hunger* and Wilson's *Space Vampires* (as *Lifeforce*) have been adapted on film. An ethically problematic vampire of a separate species, apparently owing some of his traits to both *The Vampire Tapestry* and *Fevre Dream*, appears in *Dance of the Damned* (1988) and its remake, *To Sleep with a Vampire* (1992). This nameless character (although he volunteers his name in the final scene of the later movie) is solitary, like Weyland, regarding the human species as "cattle", but like Martin's Joshua, he is cut off from his people rather than their sole survivor. The vampire of *Dance of the Damned* feeds seldom, waiting until on the verge of starvation. He chooses a stripper as his victim, a single mother contemplating suicide. The pact he offers proposes that she talk with him all night, telling him of the daylight world he has never seen, and just before dawn, he will grant her release from the burden of her life. In the course of their conversation, their relationship grows from hostility to mutuality, culminating in consensual sex and ending with the vampire's self-immolation in the glow of sunrise. Since the movie's premise requires that either vampire or human character must die--each one's survival excludes the other's--the vampire, although not supernaturally damned, can lay claim to "goodness" only by self-abnegation.

The only alien vampire story filmed for television, *Blood Ties* (1991), places its nonhuman characters near the "good" end of the moral spectrum, or, at least, no worse than the human society in which they live. The opening scenes present the unprovoked murder of a vampire couple, leaving their teenage son bereft of his parents and ignorant of his heritage. The portrayal of the vampire-hunters as homicidal fanatics predisposes the viewer toward sympathy with the vampires. The viewpoint character, Harry, a young man living a "normal" life as a reporter, exemplifies the drive to fit into mainstream society. He prefers that his people identify themselves as "Carpathian-Americans" rather than "vampires". The head of the family, on the other hand, calls Harry a "damned assimilationist" and fights against the absorption of his people into the dominant culture. At the furthest extreme from Harry, a rebellious vampire motorcycle gang flaunts their "superiority" over human beings, whom they view as existing to serve their needs. *Blood Ties* frames its vampires as just another ethnic minority, a subculture comprising both good and bad individuals like any other, deserving the same rights as any group of citizens. Attempting to make its vampires appear relatively harmless, just another minority, this film makes them almost too human. Their "extended" lifespan proves to be a modest one hundred and twenty years or so. Their present-day lifestyle apparently features only recreational blood-drinking, since they are shown eating ordinary food. They seem to have no particular aversion to daylight. In short, their creators, in making them sympathetic, sacrifice the dimension of alienness.

Yet numerous recent novels and stories we have explored demonstrate that the alien vampire can become attractive and sympathetic without losing the Otherness that generates his or her fascination. Auerbach concludes her study with "a proclamation of the end of the vampire cycle that began with revisionist eclat in the 1970s" (192). She views the vampires of the late 1980s as "suffering...loss of will" and a "lapse of initiative"; she offers the relatively new motif of the "reversibility of vampirism" as evidence that "vampirism is wearing down and vampires need a long restorative sleep" (192). She grounds this thesis, however, principally in her analysis of films such as *Near Dark, Fright Night,* and *The Lost Boys.* These movies center upon vampires of the supernatural "undead" type, all framed as evil, meriting destruction despite (or in part because of) the temptations they offer. The only "good" vampire from post-1990 print fiction discussed at length by Auerbach is the protagonist of Jewelle Gomez's *The Gilda Stories* (1991), which she characterizes as "a diluted vision of a benevolent endangered species" (184). (The term "species" is metaphorical here, though; Gilda and her followers are also defined as supernatural and therefore peripheral to our topic.) The continued proliferation of vampires, both natural and supernatural, in fiction of the mid-1990s and beyond, particularly in the juvenile and young adult categories and in the subgenre of vampire romance, suggests that Auerbach's eulogy is premature. While many of these works may prove ephemeral, like most fiction published in all genres (Sturgeon's Law remains a reliable constant), their flourishing demonstrates that the vampire motif retains its vitality in popular culture.

Vampirism remains a perennially alluring literary device because of the manifold symbolic functions it can serve, for which the "vampire as alien" is particularly well suited. Negative connotations of the alien vampire trope include disease, addiction, parasitism, invasion and infiltration threatening to exterminate or corrupt "our kind", sexual contamination and miscegenation, and the annihilation of one's identity. Though these negative motifs are most prominent in earlier works, they persist to the present, and certain elements prevalent in the present-day media hint at a shift toward the negative perception of the alien. The resurgence of the "paranoid style" manifests itself in the tags of television series such as *X-Files* ("The truth is out there") and *Dark Skies* ("History as we know it is a lie"). Nevertheless, the alien vampire theme continues to resonate with a wide range of positive associations; it facilitates the exploration of issues such as tolerance for other races, ecological responsibility, communication with intelligent beings unlike oneself, symbiosis rather than parasitism, sexual and emotional mutuality, the possibility of a new, higher species evolved or hybridized from humanity, the empowerment of the outsider, and the expansion of the self to embrace the Other. Contrary to Auerbach's suggestion that "vampirism is wearing down" (192) and Gelder's conclusion that "this subgenre is somehow already 'exhausted'" (142), I see vampires' proactive colonization of new genres in recent years--among them humor, mystery, romance, and young adult fiction--as evidence that, even while their obituary is being published, they are rising once more from the grave, like Weyland anticipating his future rebirth at the end of *The Vampire Tapestry*, as "the monster who stays true" (293).

Bibliography

This bibliography cites only fiction actually discussed in the text. It makes no attempt to be exhaustive, even as regards the works of particular authors. (For example, Lumley's Necroscope series and Smith's Night World series comprise many more volumes than those listed here.) A complete checklist of "Vampire as Alien" fiction in English would be far longer. Each January (beginning in 1990), I produce a comprehensive vampire fiction bibliography update, with classification codes identifying the types of vampires featured in each work. Annual updates are available by e-mail; contact me at MLCVamp@aol.com. For further information, see my web site: http://www.margaretlcarter.com

Primary Sources:

Aldiss, Brian. *Dracula Unbound*. New York: HarperCollins, 1991.

Benson, E. F. "Negotium Perambulans", in *Visible and Invisible*. London: Hutchinson, 1923. Rpt. in *The Collected Ghost Stories of E. F. Benson,* ed. Richard Dalby. New York: Carroll and Graf, 1992.

Bergstrom, Elaine. *Shattered Glass*. New York: Berkley, 1989.

Bixby, Jerome, and Joe E. Dean. "Share Alike". *Beyond* 1, 1 (1953). Rpt. in *Weird Vampire Tales,* ed. Robert Weinberg, et al. New York: Gramercy Books, 1992.

Blackwood, Algernon. "The Willows", in *The Listener and Other Stories*. London: Eveleigh Nash, 1907. Rpt. in *Best Ghost Stories of Algernon Blackwood,* ed. E. F. Bleiler. New York: Dover, 1975.

Bloch, Robert. "The Shambler from the Stars". *Weird Tales* 26, 3 (September 1935). Rpt. in *Mysteries of the Worm*. Oakland, CA: Chaosium, 1993.

Bradbury, Ray. "Homecoming". *Mademoiselle* (October 1946). Rpt. in *The October Country*. New York: Ballantine, 1956.
--"The Man Upstairs". *Harper's Magazine* 194 (March 1947). Rpt. in *The October Country*. New York: Ballantine, 1956.
--"Uncle Einar". 1947. Rpt. in *The October Country*. New York: Ballantine, 1956.

Brennan, M. L. *Generation V*. New York: Penguin, 2013.

Brite, Poppy Z. *Lost Souls*. New York: Delacorte, 1992.

Brown, Fredric. "Blood". *Magazine of Fantasy and Science Fiction* 8, 2 (February 1955).

Butler, Jack. *Nightshade*. New York: Atlantic Monthly Press, 1989.

Butler, Octavia. *Fledgling*. New York: Seven Stories Press, 2005.

Charnas, Suzy McKee. *Vampire Dreams*. New York: Broadway Play Publishing, 2001.
--*The Vampire Tapestry*. New York: Simon and Schuster, 1980. Rpt. New York: Pocket Books, 1981.
--and Chelsea Quinn Yarbro. "Advocates", in *Under the Fang,* ed. Robert R. McCammon. New York: Pocket Books, 1991.

Ciencin, Scott. *The Vampire Odyssey*. New York: Zebra, 1992.

Collins, Nancy A. *Sunglasses After Dark*. New York: New American Library, 1989.

Cresswell, Jasmine. *Prince of the Night*. New York: Topaz, 1995.

Farmer, Philip Jose. *Image of the Beast*. Chicago: Playboy Books, 1979. Rpt. New York: Berkley, 1985. Incorporates *Image of the Beast* (1968) and *Blown* (1969).
Gilden, Mel. *How to Be a Vampire in One Easy Lesson*. New York: Avon, 1990.
--*M Is for Monster*. New York: Avon, 1987.

Graverson, Pat. *Sweet Blood*. New York: Zebra, 1992.

Henderson, Zenna. "Food to All Flesh." *Magazine of Fantasy and Science Fiction* (1954). Rpt. in *The Anything Box*. New York: Doubleday, 1965.

Hodgman, Ann. *There's a Batwing in My Lunchbox*. New York: Avon, 1988.

Karr, Phyllis Ann. "A Cold Stake", in *Vampires,* ed. Jane Yolen and Martin H. Greenberg. New York: HarperCollins, 1991.

Kornbluth, Cyril M. "The Mindworm". *Worlds Beyond* 1 (December 1950). Rpt. in *Weird Vampire Tales,* ed. Robert Weinberg, et al. New York: Gramercy Books, 1992.

Krinard, Susan. *Prince of Dreams*. New York: Bantam, 1995.

Lee, Tanith. "Bite-Me-Not or, Fleur de Feu". *Isaac Asimov's Science Fiction Magazine* 8, 10 (October 1984). Rpt. in *Vampires,* ed. Alan Ryan. New York: Doubleday, 1987.
--*Dark Dance*. New York: Dell, 1992.
--*Sabella or The Blood Stone*. New York: DAW, 1980.

Leman, Bob. "The Pilgrimage of Clifford M". *Magazine of Fantasy and Science Fiction* 66, 5 (May 1984), 8-30.

Lewis, C. S. *Out of the Silent Planet*. London: John Lane, 1938. Rpt. New York: Macmillan, 1965.

Lichtenberg, Jacqueline. *House of Zeor.* New York: Doubleday, 1974. Rpt. New York: Pocket Books, 1977.

--*Those of My Blood.* New York: St. Martin's, 1988.

Long, Frank Belknap, Jr. "The Horror from the Hills". *Weird Tales* 17, 1-2 (January-March 1931). Rpt. Sauk City, WI: Arkham House, 1963. Rpt. in *Odd Science Fiction.* New York: Belmont, 1964.

Lovecraft, H. P. "The Dunwich Horror". *Weird Tales* 13, 4 (April 1929). Rpt. in *The Dunwich Horror and Others.* Sauk City, WI: Arkham House, 1939. Rpt. New York: Lancer, 1963.

--"The Shunned House." *Weird Tales* 30, 4 (October 1937). Rpt. in *At the Mountains of Madness and Other Tales of Terror.* New York: Beagle Books, 1971.

Lumley, Brian. *Blood Brothers.* New York: Tor, 1992.

--*Necroscope.* New York: Tor, 1988.

--*The Source.* New York: Tor, 1989.

McDowell, Michael. "Halley's Passing". *Twilight Zone* 7, 2 (June 1989).

MacEwen, P. H. "A Winter's Night", in *Writers of the Future, Volume IV,* ed. Algis Budrys. Los Angeles: Bridge Publications, 1988.

Martin, George R. R. *Fevre Dream.* New York: Simon and Schuster, 1982.

Matheson, Richard. "Dress of White Silk". *Magazine of Fantasy and Science Fiction* 2, 5 (1951). Rpt. in *Vamps,* ed. Martin H. Greenberg and Charles G. Waugh. New York: DAW, 1987.

--"Drink My Red Blood". *Imagination* 2, 2 (April 1951). Rpt. as "Drink My Blood" in *The Midnight People,* ed. Peter Haining. London: Leslie Frewin, 1968.

--*I Am Legend.* New York: Fawcett, 1954.

Maupassant, Guy de. "Le Horla". *Gil Blas* (26 October 1886). Rpt. Paris: Paul Ollendorff, 1887. Trans. Marjorie Laurie and rpt. as "The Horla" in *The Vampire,* ed. Ornella Volta and Valeria Riva. London: Neville Spearman Ltd., 1963.

Moore, C. L. "Shambleau". *Weird Tales* 22, 5 (November 1933). Rpt. in *Weird Vampire Tales,* ed. Robert Weinberg, et al. New York: Gramercy Books, 1992.

Navarro, Yvonne. *AfterAge.* New York: Bantam, 1993.

Newman, Kim. *Bad Dreams.* London: Simon and Schuster, 1990. Rpt. New York: Carroll and Graf, 1991.

O'Brien, Fitz-James. "What Was It? A Mystery". *Harper's New Monthly Magazine* (March 1859). Rpt. in *The Supernatural Tales of Fitz-James O'Brien: Volume One: Macabre Tales,* ed. Jessica Amanda Salmonson. New York: Doubleday, 1988.

Petrey, Susan. "The Healer's Touch". *Magazine of Fantasy and Science Fiction* 62, 2 (February 1982). Rpt. in *Gifts of Blood.* New York: Baen, 1992.

--"Leechcraft". *Magazine of Fantasy and Science Fiction* 62, 5 (May 1982). Rpt. in *Gifts of Blood.* New York: Baen, 1992.

Powers, Tim. *The Stress of Her Regard.* Lynbrook, NY: Charnel House, 1989. Rpt. New York: Ace, 1991.

Ptacek, Kathryn. *Blood Autumn.* New York: Tor, 1985.
--*In Silence Sealed.* New York: Tor, 1988.

Rein-Hagen, Mark, ed. *Book of the Kindred.* Clarkston, GA: White Wolf, 1996.

Relling, William, Jr. "The Obsession", in *The Bradbury Chronicles,* ed. William F. Nolan and Martin H. Greenberg. New York: Penguin, 1991.

Robinson, Phil. "The Last of the Vampires". *The Contemporary Review* 63 (March 1893). Rpt. in *Vampire*, ed. Peter Haining. London: Severn House Publishers, 1985.

Rusch, Kristine Kathryn. *Sins of the Blood.* New York: Dell, 1994.
--"Victims", in *Sisters of the Night,* ed. Barbara Hambly and Martin H. Greenberg. New York: Warner Books, 1995.

Russell, Eric Frank. *Sinister Barrier. Unknown* (March 1939). Rpt. Reading, PA: Fantasy Press, 1948.

Scott, Jody. *I, Vampire.* New York: Ace, 1984.

Simmons, Dan. *Children of the Night.* New York: G. P. Putnam's Sons, 1992.
--"Dying in Bangkok", in *Lovedeath.* New York: Warner, 1993. Revised reprint of "Death in Bangkok." *Playboy* (June 1993).

Smith, L. J. *Daughters of Darkness*. New York: Pocket Books, 1996.
--*Secret Vampire*. New York: Pocket Books, 1996.

Spruill, Steven. *Rulers of Darkness*. New York: St. Martin's, 1995.

Stableford, Brian. *The Empire of Fear*. UK: Simon and Schuster, 1988.
--"The Hunger and Ecstasy of Vampires". *Interzone* (January/February 1995). Rpt. in *Virtuous Vampires*, ed. Stefan Dziemianowicz, et al. New York: Barnes and Noble, 1996.

Stirling, S. M. *The Council of Shadows*. New York: New American Library, 2011.
-- *Shadows of Falling Night*. New York: New American Library, 2013.
-- *A Taint in the Blood*. New York: New American Library, 2010.

Stoker, Bram. *Dracula*. Westminster: A. Constable, 1897. Rpt. as *The Essential Dracula*, ed. Leonard Wolf. New York: Penguin, 1993.

Straum, Niel. "Vanishing Breed", in *Curse of the Undead*, ed. M. L. Carter. New York: Fawcett, 1970. Revised rpt. as by "Leslie Roy Carter" in *Tomorrow Sucks*, ed. Greg Cox and T. K. Weisskopf. New York: Baen, 1994.

Strieber, Whitley. *The Hunger*. New York: William Morrow, 1981.

Tem, Melanie. *Desmodus*. New York: Dell, 1995.

Tenn, William. "The Human Angle". *Famous Fantastic Mysteries* (1948). Rpt. in *The Human Angle*. New York: Ballantine, 1956.

--"She Only Goes Out at Night". *Fantastic Universe* 6, 3 (1956). Rpt. in *Weird Vampire Tales,* ed. Robert Weinberg, et al. New York: Gramercy Books, 1992.

Tiptree, James, Jr. "And I Awoke and Found Me Here on the Cold Hill's Side". 1971. Rpt. in *Ten Thousand Light Years from Home.* New York: Ace, 1973.

Van Vogt, A. E. "Asylum". *Astounding Science Fiction* 29, 3 (May 1942).
--"The Proxy Intelligence". *Worlds of If* 18, 10 (October 1968).

Ward, J. R. *Dark Lover.* New York: Signet, 2005.

Wells, H. G. *The War of the Worlds.* London: William Heinemann, 1898. Rpt. in *Seven Science Fiction Novels of H. G. Wells.* New York: Dover, 1950.

Williamson, Jack. *Darker Than You Think. Unknown* 4, 4 (December 1940). Rpt. New York: Berkley, 1969.

Wilson, Colin. *The Mind Parasites.* Sauk City, WI: Arkham House, 1967. Rpt. New York: Bantam, 1968.
--*The Philosopher's Stone.* New York: Crown Publishers, 1969. Rpt. New York: Warner, 1974.
--*The Space Vampires.* New York: Random House, 1976. Rpt. New York: Pocket Books, 1977.

Yarbro, Chelsea Quinn. *The Saint-Germain Chronicles.* New York: Pocket Books, 1983.
--"Salome", in *The Bradbury Chronicles,* ed. William F. Nolan and Martin H. Greenberg. New York: Penguin, 1991.

Secondary Sources:

Auerbach, Nina. *Our Vampires, Ourselves.* Chicago: University of Chicago Press, 1995.

Barr, Marleen. "Holding Fast to Feminism and Moving Beyond: Suzy McKee Charnas's *The Vampire Tapestry*", in *The Feminine Eye,* ed. Tom Staicar. New York: Frederick Ungar, 1982.

Carter, Margaret L. "Interview with Suzy McKee Charnas". *The Vampire's Crypt* 2 (Summer 1990): 3-10.

Cranny-Francis, Anne. "De-Fanging the Vampire: S. M. Charnas' *The Vampire Tapestry* as Subversive Horror", in *American Horror Fiction: From Brockden Brown to Stephen King.* New York: St. Martin's, 1990.

Dansky, Richard E. "Transgression, Spheres of Influence, and the Use of the Utterly Other in Lovecraft". *Lovecraft Studies* 30 (Spring 1994): 5-14.

Dingley, R. J. "Count Dracula and the Martians", in *The Victorian Fantasists,* ed. Kath Filmer. New York: St. Martin's, 1991.

Dziemianowicz, Stefan. "'The Green Meadow' and 'The Willows': Lovecraft, Blackwood, and a Peculiar Coincidence". *Lovecraft Studies* 19/20 (Fall 1989): 33-39.

Gelder, Ken. *Reading the Vampire.* New York: Routledge, 1994.

Gordon, Joan. "Rehabilitating Revenants, or Sympathetic Vampires in Recent Fiction." *Extrapolation* 29, 3 (1988): 227-234.

Griffin, Gail B. "'Your Girls That You All Love Are Mine': *Dracula* and the Victorian Male Sexual Imagination.." *International Journal of Women's Studies* 3, 5 (1980): 454-465. Rpt. in *Dracula: The Vampire and the Critics,* ed. Margaret L. Carter. Ann Arbor: UMI Research Press, 1988.

Hofstadter, Richard. "The Paranoid Style in American Politics", in *The Paranoid Style in American Politics and Other Essays.* New York: Knopf, 1965.

Hollinger, Veronica. "The Vampire and/as the Alien". *Journal of the Fantastic in the Arts* 5, 3 (1993): 5-17.

Hume, Kathryn. "The Hidden Dynamics of *The War of the Worlds*". *Philological Quarterly* 62, 3 (Summer, 1983): 279-292.

Huntington, John. *The Logic of Fantasy: H. G. Wells and Science Fiction.* New York: Columbia University Press, 1982.

Jackson, Rosemary. *Fantasy: The Literature of Subversion.* New York: Methuen, 1981.

Jameson, Fredric. "Magical Narratives: Romance as Genre". *New Literary History* 7 (1975): 135-163.

Johnson, Judith E. "Women and Vampires: Nightmare or Utopia?" *The Kenyon Review* 15, 1 (Winter 1993): 72-80.

Jones, Ernest. *On the Nightmare.* 1931. Rpt. New York: Liveright, 1951.

King, Maureen. "Contemporary Women Writers and the 'New Evil': The Vampires of Anne Rice and Suzy McKee Charnas". *Journal of the Fantastic in the Arts* 5, 3 (1993): 75-84.

Lem, Stanislaus. "H. G. Wells' *The War of the Worlds*", trans. John Coutouvidis, in *Science Fiction Roots and Branches,* ed. Rhys Garnett and R. J. Ellis. New York: St. Martin's, 1990.

Lewis, C. S. "Unreal Estates". *SF Horizons* (Spring 1964). Rpt. in *On Stories and Other Essays in Literature,* ed. Walter Hooper. New York: Harcourt Brace Jovanovich, 1982.

Lichtenberg, Jacqueline. "The 'Kill/Need' Convention". *Ambrov Zeor* 22 (May 1993): 6-7.
--"A Proposal for a New Genre Name". *Ambrov Zeor* 22 (May 1993): 68-73.
--"Vampire with Muddy Boots". *Onyx* 1, 3 (February 1992): 4-6.

Martin, Anya. "A Conversation with Anne Rice". *Cemetery Dance* 3, 3 (Summer 1991): 34-39.

Melton, J. Gordon. "The Vegetarian Vampire: On Introducing Dracula to Children". *Transylvanian Journal* 2, 1 (Spring/Summer 1996): 17-30.

Mosig, Dirk W. "H. P. Lovecraft: Myth-Maker". *The Miskatonic* (February 1976). Rpt. in *H. P. Lovecraft: Four Decades of Criticism,* ed. S. T. Joshi. Athens, OH: Ohio University Press, 1980.

Prince, Gerald. "'Le Horla,' Sex, and Colonization", in *Alteratives,* ed. Warren Motte and Gerald Prince. Lexington, KY: French Forum Publishers, 1993.
Ramsland, Katherine. *The Vampire Companion: The Official Guide to Anne Rice's The Vampire Chronicles.* Second Edition. New York: Ballantine, 1995.

Riley, Michael. *Conversations with Anne Rice.* New York: Ballantine, 1996.

Senf, Carol A. "*Dracula:* The Unseen Face in the Mirror". *Journal of Narrative Technique* 9 (1979): 160-170. Rpt. in *Dracula: The Vampire and the Critics,* ed. Margaret L. Carter. Ann Arbor: UMI Research Press, 1988.
--*The Vampire in Nineteenth-Century English Literature.* Bowling Green, OH: Popular Press, 1988.

Siebers, Tobin. *The Romantic Fantastic.* Ithaca, NY: Cornell University Press, 1984.

Simpson, Anne B. "The 'Tangible Antagonist': H. G. Wells and the Discourse of Otherness". *Extrapolation* 31, 2 (Summer 1990): 134-147.

Skal, David J. *The Monster Show: A Cultural History of Horror.* New York: W. W. Norton, 1991.
--*V Is for Vampire.* New York: Penguin, 1996.

Stevenson, John Allan. "A Vampire in the Mirror: The Sexuality of *Dracula*". *PMLA* 103, 2 (1988): 139-149.

Taylor, Shawn. *Parables, Vampires, and Pregnant Men: The Narrative Resistance of Octavia E. Butler.* Amazon Digital Services (http://www.amazon.com), 2017.

Timpone, Anthony, ed. *Fangoria Vampires.* New York: HarperPrism, 1996.

Tolkien, J. R. R. "On Fairy-Stories". 1964. Rpt. in *The Tolkien Reader.* New York: Ballantine, 1966.

Warner, Marina. *From the Beast to the Blonde: On Fairy Tales and Their Tellers.* London: Chatto and Windus, 1994. Rpt. New York: Farrar, Straus, and Giroux, 1994.

Wilgus, Neal. "Saberhagen's New Dracula: The Vampire as Hero", in *Discovering Modern Horror Fiction,* ed. Darrell Schweitzer. Mercer Island, WA: Starmont House, 1985.

Checklist of Authors and Critics,

WITH Chapter WHERE FIRST MENTIONED

These checklists are offered in lieu of an index because the differences in page numbering among various editions make conventional indexing impractical.

Aldiss, Brian (4)

Auerbach, Nina (1)

Barr, Marleen (3)

Benson, E. F. (1)

Bergstrom, Elaine (3)

Bixby, Jerome (2)

Blackwood, Algernon (1)

Bloch, Robert (2)

Bradbury, Ray (2)

Brennan, M. L. (3)

Brite, Poppy Z. (4)

Brown, Fredric (2)

Butler, Jack (3)

Butler, Octavia (3)

Charnas, Suzy McKee (3)

Ciencin, Scott (4)

Cranny-Francis, Anne (3)

Collins, Nancy A. (3)

Yarbro, Chelsea Quinn (Introduction)

Checklist of Fiction and Film Titles,

WITH Chapter WHERE FIRST MENTIONED

Note: It is not feasible to provide page numbers, because of different pagination among various formats of the book.)

"Advocates" (4)

AfterAge (2)

"And I Awoke and Found Me Here on the Cold Hill's Side" (Introduction)

"Asylum" (2)

Bad Dreams (4)

"Bite-Me-Not or, Fleur de Feu" (3)

"Blood" (2)

Blood Brothers (4)

Blood Ties (Conclusion)

The Body Snatchers (2)

Book of the Kindred (Conclusion)

Buffy the Vampire Slayer (Conclusion)

Children of the Night *(3)*

"A Cold Stake" (3)

Dance of the Damned (Conclusion)

Dark Dance (3)

Dark Lover (3)

Dark Prince (3)

You can find ALL our books up on our website at:

http://www.writers-exchange.com

All our Non-Fiction:

http://www.writers-exchange.com/category/genres/nonfiction/

All Margaret's Books:

http://www.writers-exchange.com/Margaret-Carter/

About the Author

Marked for life by reading *Dracula* at the age of twelve, Margaret L. Carter specializes in the literature of fantasy and the supernatural, particularly vampires. She received degrees in English from the College of William and Mary, the University of Hawaii, and the University of California, with her dissertation published as *Specter or Delusion? The Supernatural in Gothic Fiction*. Her other works include *Dracula: The Vampire and the Critics*, *The Vampire In Literature: A Critical Bibliography*, and *Different Blood: The Vampire As Alien*. She is also the author of a werewolf novel, *Shadow Of The Beast*, and four vampire novels, *Dark Changeling* (2000 Eppie Award winner in Horror), *Child Of Twilight*, *Sealed In Blood*, and *Crimson Dreams*, along with a fantasy novel, *Wild Sorceress*, co-written by her husband Les Carter, and a horror novel, *From The Dark Places*.

Margaret and Les, a retired Navy Captain, have four sons and several grandchildren. For fans of "Vamp Tales", please do not hesitate to visit her website: The Vampire's Crypt at:

http://www.margaretlcarter.com/

You can keep track of all Margaret's books on her author page at Writers Exchange E-Publishing:

http://www.writers-exchange.com/Margaret-Carter/

If you enjoyed this author's book, then please place a review up at the site of purchase, and any social media sites you frequent!

If you want to read more about books by this author, they are listed on the following pages...

Crimson Dreams

The summer when Heather was eighteen, her dream beast's nightly visits warded off loneliness and swept her away in flights of ecstasy. Now, returning to the mountains to sell her dead parents' vacation cabin, she finds her "beast" again. But he turns out to be more than a dream. She meets Devin in the flesh, apparently not a day older. His first human lover, centuries in the past, died horribly because of her devotion to him. Does he dare expose another mortal woman to that risk?

Publisher: http://www.writers-exchange.com/Crimson-Dreams/

Different Blood: The Vampire as Alien

Different blood flows in their veins--but our blood quenches their thirst. From Bram Stoker's 1897 creation of Count Dracula, portrayed as a foreign invader bent on the conquest of England, the literary vampire has symbolized the Other, whether his or her otherness arises from racial, ethnic, sexual, or species difference. Even before the bloodsucking Martians of H. G. Wells' *War of the Worlds*, however, popular fiction contained a few vampires who were members of alien species rather than supernatural undead.

Even more intriguing than interplanetary invaders are humanoid and quasi-humanoid beings who have evolved to live on Earth among us, often camouflaged as our own kind. The boom in vampire fiction that began in the 1970s engendered a variety of "alien" vampires, many of them portrayed as sympathetic characters. The science fiction vampire is especially suited to the presentation of vampirism as morally neutral rather than inherently evil.

Different Blood surveys the literary vampire as alien, whether extraterrestrial or a different species evolved on Earth, from the mid-1800s to the 1990s, and analyzes the many uses to which science fiction and fantasy authors have put this theme. Their works explore issues of species, race, ecological responsibility, gender, eroticism, xenophobia, parasitism, symbiosis, intimacy, and the bridging of differences. An extensive bibliography lists dozens of novels and short stories on the "vampire as alien" theme, many of which are still in print.

Publisher: http://www.writers-exchange.com/Different-Blood/

From the Dark Places and Against the Dark Devourer

From the Dark Places

When Father Michel Emeric and Dr. Ray Benson warn young widow Kate Jacobs of occult danger stalking her, she dismisses them as deranged fanatics. The eerie disappearance of her four-year-old daughter, Sara, changes her mind. Ray and Father Mike rescue Kate's child, but the fight has only begun. Dark powers from beyond our world want to destroy Kate and Sara and prevent the birth of a future child foretold to have extraordinary psychic powers and a destiny as a great warrior against evil. Kate must develop her latent wild talents and allow Sara to do the same, in a universe weirder--and more dangerous-- than she's ever imagined.

Publisher: http://www.writers-exchange.com/From-the-Dark-Places/

Against the Dark Devourer (Sequel to From the Dark Places)

All her life, Deborah has known she and her older sister have extraordinary psi powers. When their mother dies suddenly, Deborah learns she's meant to use her gift against the forces of darkness in some special way. How, she doesn't have a clue, but she wants no part of this alleged fate. Yet with evil forces stalking her, can she avoid the battle ahead?

All his life, Victor has known he and his twin sister have a unique destiny. Bred to serve inhuman entities from another dimensional plane, he's instructed to either seduce a strange young woman who poses a grave threat to the cult he belongs to...or destroy her.

Unexpectedly, he finds Deborah not only attractive and intelligent but his equal in psychic power. Although his cult views religion with contempt--and she's an unabashed Christian--he's helplessly drawn to her. For her part, Deborah finds in Victor a kindred spirit. For the first time, someone other than her sister can empathize with her differences from "normal" people. Is prophetic destiny written in stone, even for two potential foes falling in love? A paranormal romance inspired by C. S. Lewis's *That Hideous Strength* and the cosmic horror of H. P. Lovecraft.

Publisher: http://www.writers-exchange.com/Against-the-Dark-Devourer/

Heart's Desires and Dark Embraces

When Margaret L. Carter first read *Dracula* at the age of twelve, her spontaneous reaction was to wonder how the undead Count saw the events in which he was portrayed as the villain. She's always been fascinated with the "monster's" viewpoint and relationships between human and nonhuman beings. Most of the stories in this collection can be described as romances, and all involve love and passion in some form. Here you'll encounter vampires, elves, ghosts, and at least one human-monster hybrid. The vampire stories in the first half of the book are part of an ongoing series in which the creatures we know as vampires belong to a naturally evolved, nonhuman species secretly living among us. Readers can get better acquainted with them in *Crimson Dreams, Sealed in Blood,* and *Passion in the Blood.*

Publisher: http://www.writers-exchange.com/Hearts-Desires-and-Dark-Embraces/

Passion in the Blood

Cordelia and her twin sister don't realize the mother who left them soon after their birth bequeathed them a dark bloodline. They're half vampire. Although human in most respects, they possess certain psychic gifts. A friend of their late father's, Karl, also a vampire, has been watching over their family for generations in honor of his love for their distant ancestor. When her sister is kidnapped and Cordelia must beg for help from Karl, she learns the truth about his vampirism and her own heritage. In the process, she and Karl form a blood bond that leads to deeper intimacy than either one could have anticipated.

Publisher: http://www.writers-exchange.com/Passion-in-the-Blood/

Sealed in Blood

Science fiction conventions attract some strange people, but Sherri Hudson never expected to spend a con weekend helping a sexy man in a cape steal photos of a winged alien. When the photographer is murdered and Nigel Jamison reveals to Sherri that the "alien" is actually his sister, the situation gets intriguingly complicated. Unwillingly swept up in Nigel's quest to rescue his sister, Sherri can't help being fascinated with him. By the time she finds out he's a vampire, the fascination has become mutual--and too strong to resist.

Publisher: http://www.writers-exchange.com/sealed-in-blood/

Sealing the Dark Portal

Almost nothing Rina remembers about her life is true. Rather than the ordinary librarian she believes herself to be, she's actually a sorceress who fled from another world to ours when creatures from an alien dimension devastated her home and killed her family. Now they've pursued her to our world, summoned by a sorcerer who plans to open a portal and invite monstrous entities from the void between dimensions to overrun this planet. Rina's former bodyguard, a cat shapeshifter who was once her lover and still yearns for her, helps her true memories to awaken. She must come to terms with the truth about her past so that together they can save their new home from the fate of their old one.

Publisher: http://www.writers-exchange.com/sealing-the-dark-portal/

Shadow of the Beast

After the mysterious deaths of her brother and sister at the fangs of what looks like a feral dog, Jenny Cameron develops nightmares and blackouts. The quest for the truth about herself leads to her long-lost father, who deserted the family before her birth. He seeks redemption for the curse he carries, but has his bloody past condemned him beyond salvation? When Jenny discovers the secret of her dark heritage, she's no longer sure she can trust her dangerous nature enough to be with the man she loves, and she may ultimately be forced to destroy her own father. Fearing she has inherited the violence that rages in him, she struggles to find her true self under the shadow of the beast.

Publisher: http://www.writers-exchange.com/Shadow-of-the-Beast/

Wild Sorceress Series
By Margaret L. Carter and Leslie Roy Carter

In a world where hostile nations wield magic in combat, twin sorceresses separated at birth and brought up on opposing sides of the war find each other. Together, they face persecution for using wild magic, fight against traitors and assassins, explore family secrets, and discover the hidden origins of magic itself. Above all, to protect their world, they must deal with ancient, powerful dragons that most people don't even believe exist.

Prequel: Legacy of Magic

Most people in the country of Saphradea admire sorcerers and dream of having magical powers. Not Merina, a young woman who detests magic because she thinks it ruined the life of her mother, a failed sorceress candidate who abandoned her in infancy.

When Merina's fiance, Trinames, announces he's decided to go for training as a Healer sorcerer, her personal world turns upside down. Merina is heiress to a tract of rich farmland, and she wants only to manage her own property and bring up a family in peace--a dream she thought Trinames shared. Yet events conspire to force her into a realm of magic and intrigue she never wanted.

When Trinames is kidnapped and she strikes out across the wilderness to rescue him, in company with a wandering trader who turns out to be more than he appears, she runs into a crisis that awakens magical powers she shouldn't even possess.

Publisher: http://www.writers-exchange.com/Legacy-of-Magic/

Book 1: Wild Sorceress

In a world where warring nations use magic in combat, years ago young sorceress Aetria's untamed power caused a disaster on the battlefield. Temporarily banished and retrained, she's returned to the army to redeem herself as head of a company of novice mages. She uncovers a traitorous plot by her own commander, renews her bond with her "imaginary" childhood friend, and meets her long-lost twin sister. While also becoming a trusted friend of the commanding general of the army, Aetria unearths secrets of the true nature of the magic she and her comrades wield.

Publisher: http://www.writers-exchange.com/Wild-Sorceress/

Book 2: Besieged Adept

While learning to control her wild sorcery, Adept Aetria has defeated a pair of traitors trying to kill her, found a long-lost twin, and uncovered secrets of the source and nature of magic. Now she continues her research while battling the remnants of the Neo-Aggressor rebellion and integrating raw, untrained talent into the Sorcerer Corps. Meanwhile, she discovers deeper secrets of her own family background, along with a surprising new foe and a destiny she never dreamed of. Furthermore, she learns that her "imaginary" dragon friend Rajii actually exists...but so do less friendly dragons. What does their agenda mean for the future of humanity and magic in Aetria's world?

Publisher: http://www.writers-exchange.com/Besieged-Adept/

Book 3: Rogue Magess

Sorceresses Aetria and Coleni discover that both their own births and the history of their world have been manipulated in secret by an ancient, powerful race of dragons. Some, like Aetria's lifelong friend Rajii, have benevolent intentions toward humanity while others want to restore the people of the Domains to total slavery. All, however, have their own agendas with human beings and mortal magic as pawns.

Emerging from their long-lost mother's hidden home in the deserted Non-Lands, Aetria and Coleni find themselves targeted by assassins under control of the dragons. While the sisters' powers continue to grow, so do the magical gifts of Coleni's baby daughter, but will their magic provide adequate protection?

Meanwhile, still viewed with suspicion for their "wild sorcery", they can't convince most of their rivals and allies, including Aetria's old mentor and the commanding general of the army, that the dragons and the danger they pose are real.

Publisher: http://www.writers-exchange.com/Rogue-Magess/

Windwalker's Mate

Shannon's little boy Daniel has disturbing psychic powers. He talks to the wind--and it listens. All Shannon wants is a normal life. She wants to forget the cult of the Windwalker, a dark god from another dimension, and the terrifying night when her child was conceived. But her first love, Nathan, son of the cult leader, contacts her for the first time since that horrific ceremony. He claims his father is stalking Shannon and Daniel. Whose child is Daniel, Nathan's or the Windwalker's? Nathan's father plans to use Daniel to open a gate between dimensions and unleash chaos on our world. To save her child and become reconciled with her first love, Shannon may have no choice but embrace the strange powers she previously rejected.

Publisher: http://www.writers-exchange.com/windwalkers-mate/

You can find ALL our books up on our website at:

http://www.writers-exchange.com

All our Non-Fiction:

http://www.writers-exchange.com/category/genres/nonfiction/

All Margaret's Books:

http://www.writers-exchange.com/Margaret-Carter/